BEYOND CURRY INDIAN COOKBOOK

Beyond Curry
INDIAN COOKBOOK

A Culinary Journey Through India

Denise D'silva Sankhé

ROCKRIDGE
PRESS

To Prasanna,

For partnering with me in gluttony. For introducing me to "escape velocity." For giving me wings. Sharing this one life and its little journeys with you is my greatest blessing. (Clooney just didn't make the cut.)

For general information on our other products and services or to obtain technical support, please contact our Customer Care Department within the United States at (866) 744-2665, or outside the United States at (510) 253-0500.

Rockridge Press publishes its books in a variety of electronic and print formats. Some content that appears in print may not be available in electronic books, and vice versa.

ISBN: 978-1-62315-696-1
eBook 978-1-62315-697-8

A Culinary Adventure
THROUGH THE WORLD OF AUTHENTIC INDIAN FOOD

Arm yourself with the secrets behind authentic Indian food and get to know tips and tricks that will simplify the cuisine for your kitchen and your dining table.

The journey begins in the North ❶ with classics like Tandoori Chicken (page 168) and Carrot Halva (page 231).

Move on to the Northeast ❷ with the delicious flavors of Naga Pork with Bamboo Shoots (page 178) and Tangy Assamese Fish Curry (page 203).

Stop over in the East ❸ for lovely seafood delicacies like Shrimp in Coconut Cream Sauce (page 214) and Bengali Fish Croquettes (page 66).

Head to the beautiful South ❹ for breakfast delights like Easy Rice and Lentil Crêpes (page 97) or the popular Hyderabadi Lamb Biryani (page 83).

End your adventure in West and Central India ❺ with Goan Shrimp and Okra Curry (page 211) or Tangy Whole Red Lentils (page 150).

Also included are popular Indian fusion dishes, like the Chinese-inspired Manchurian Fish (page 209) and British-inspired Crumb-Fried Mutton Chops (page 70), as well as everyday staples like Plain Naan (page 92) and Millet Pilaf (page 88).

CONTENTS

INTRODUCTION

I was born and raised in Bombay (now Mumbai), one of the most cosmopolitan cities in India. Rich in history, the city shows signs of its early colonization, as well as more recent changes from the growing migrant population hailing from all regions of India—everyone living, sharing, and blending into a fascinating ethnic mosaic. My own cultural background mirrors the melting pot of the city, with half my family being Anglo-Indian (a small community of British colonial rulers who married into the Indian community and formed a new subculture) and half being Mangalorean (natives of a seaside district in Southern India). Just to make the mix more interesting, I grew up alongside a variety of religious communities and married a Hindu. Suffice it to say, this wonderful intermingling puts beautiful food on the table.

As a child, ironically, I ran away from food. I'd sneak away and throw a bitter tantrum only to be reminded that food can never be wasted. Indians at home firmly believe that food is akin to God—and what's on your plate *must* be eaten. So when I was a child, my grandfather would sit me down on his lap and read me stories while giving me the freedom to mix my morsels more creatively as I listened. This broke a barrier for me as I could combine the various courses on my plate any way I wanted to. And just as I reacted with pleasure to the stories being read to me, I would be pleasantly surprised by the end results with my food.

This was the early beginning of my love for eating and experimenting with the wonderful array of spices and produce that India has to offer. I began to deeply love and pursue authentic Indian food in all its diversity, and eventually write about it on one of the leading food blogs of the world, Serious Eats.

In the course of writing my column *Beyond Curry*, I came to realize that there's a growing, global interest in Indian food. I would get emails from Indian expats and non-Indians alike, many asking questions about cooking techniques or thanking me for bringing authentic Indian flavors to their cooking. I loved hearing from Indian readers who said my recipes reminded them of a trip they took back home or evoked memories of a dish made by a loved granny who was no longer with them. That's what Indian food does—it takes you on a journey, one that is sometimes sensorial and sometimes nostalgic.

Nowhere in the world is diversity more a fact of life than in India. And nowhere are the stories of a people and a religion more apparent than in their food. Indians speak more than 50 different languages, and with all religions combined, worship more than a billion gods. You can imagine how varied and interesting the cuisine can be with this amazing mix. In fact, there is a saying that the simple lentil dish dal, which is commonly eaten across India, changes in texture, taste, and flavor every 200 meters. That is the beauty of Indian regional food. And that is the fantastic journey I intend to take you on through the pages of this book.

My connection with Indian spices and flavors helps me use my knowledge in the modern kitchen. Without sacrificing authenticity, I use updated cooking methods with modern appliances to create delicious Indian food. Come with me on a journey of nostalgia, discovery, and surprises that only a cuisine as diverse as India's can take you on. If you are an Indian living outside the country, many of these recipes will bring back memories of your own childhood or meals cooked at festivals. If you're new to Indian food, this will be like a storybook discovery of a cuisine that is hearty and diverse.

A common misconception is that Indian food is difficult to make, based on the sheer number of ingredients needed for a recipe. But Indians eat home-cooked food three meals a day, so it really can't be that difficult. To help you become more confident, this book is full of helpful tips on stocking an Indian pantry, handy time-savers, and of course, simple, authentic recipes that will make you fall in love with India's foods as passionately as I have.

1

VARIETY, THE SPICE OF LIFE

To many in the West, Indian food is synonymous with burning-the-taste-buds heat, but this couldn't be farther from the truth. While the cuisine is rich in spices and bold flavors, it is also hinged on balance and subtlety. The Indian diet is one of the most balanced in the world, with every food group thoughtfully represented in each meal.

Food is at the center of our culture. It is not only a part of festivals and important life occasions, but its ingredients are also believed to be of therapeutic value. Food is worshipped and treated with great respect and love.

MORE THAN JUST MASALAS

With a history that dates back to the Indus Valley civilization, Indian food has come a long and interesting way. India has seen many rulers, settlers, and colonizers. Many of them have left an indelible mark on our cuisine, with perhaps the most prominent culinary legacy being that of the Central Asian Mughals. India was largely vegetarian before their arrival. When the Mughals invaded from the north, they brought with them their style of Persian-influenced cooking, which was rich in ingredients such as dried fruit, grilled meats, and robust whole spices. The food of North India still mirrors this today.

Indian staples like chiles, potatoes, and tomatoes were actually introduced by the Portuguese when they colonized the western states of India in the 15th century. Their culinary influences combined with native Indian dishes and ingredients to create classics like pork vindaloo.

India was a prominent supplier of spices on the historic Spice Route that connected the Eastern and Western worlds. This intermingling gave rise to even richer and more diverse culinary traditions. The French and Dutch both colonized small areas in India, but of the two, only French influences can still be seen in the cuisine of Pondicherry in South India.

The British, who ruled India for over 200 years, mellowed the spice levels in our dishes, introduced new methods of cooking, and made tea (chai) a household necessity. Before independence, British colonizers attempted to oversimplify Indian food by simply calling it curry. But, in fact, Indian food is so much more. Curry, to most Indians, is only one type of dish, a gravy- or sauce-based one, which can have meat or vegetables in it.

Other groups that have contributed to India's culinary landscape are the Jews, the Parsis, and the Chinese. Each of these communities brought with them their customs and their food. And in typical Indian fashion, we accepted and assimilated these dishes into the mainstream.

Another layer in the tapestry of Indian cuisine is the range of religious tenets governing food. Some religions forbid animal protein and root vegetables, some are vegan, and others allow only certain meats. This has resulted in even more resourcefulness with ingredients, and, ironically, more variety within the restrictions.

Modern India has taken the best of all these influences and emerged with a cuisine that is as diverse as it is unique. Indian food is difficult to describe in one sentence, simply because of its variety. In a land of many cultures, climates, and languages, Indian food is beautifully rich and unique. While cooking styles are similar throughout the subcontinent, the resulting dishes, even if they have the same name, differ in taste and flavor from one region to another.

A FEAST OF REGIONAL FLAVORS AND FAVORITES

My travels through the most populous states and the most obscure little villages in India have given me plenty of material for this book. As you take this journey with me, I hope to open your eyes to the bounty of Indian regional food. Indian food can be broadly classified into North, Northeast, West and Central, South (or Southeast), and East. The geography, climate, and external influences of a region greatly define the kind of food that is eaten.

Starting the journey in the North, which has extreme winters, hilly terrain, and an agrarian economy, as in the Punjab, you will find more robust dishes. Wheat, lentils, and spices are staples, and dairy products are ubiquitous. Here, oil and ghee (clarified butter) are used more generously, and the food is rich, wholesome, and varied in both the meats and vegetables used.

The Northeast is a stark contrast, with more fresh spices and herbs in the cuisine. This part of India is still quite disconnected from the rest of the country in terms of geography, and the states here—Arunachal Pradesh, Assam, Nagaland, Manipur, Mizoram, Tripura, and Meghalaya, endearingly known as the Seven Sisters, as well as Sikkim farther north—have a cuisine that is completely distinct from mainstream Indian food. The area is dominated by different tribal communities, with influences from bordering Bhutan, Burma, and China. Pork and fish are the meats favored in this region, and rice is served at every meal.

In the West, seafood becomes more prominent along the coastal belt, and vegetarianism is predominant in states like Gujarat. Central India borrows from all its neighboring regions. Here you can enjoy the mouthwatering array of snacks (chaat) made from staples such as corn, maize, millet, and sorghum. This area is also home to a wide array of milk-based dishes and pickles.

India's Regions and States

NORTH Jammu and Kashmir
Punjab ◆ Haryana ◆ Delhi
Uttar Pradesh ◆ Rajasthan
Uttarakhand ◆ Chandigarh
Himachal Pradesh

NORTHEAST Arunachal Pradesh
Assam ◆ Manipur ◆ Meghalaya
Mizoram ◆ Nagaland ◆ Tripura
Sikkim

EAST Bihar ◆ West Bengal
Orissa

WEST AND CENTRAL
Gujarat ◆ Daman and Diu
Dadra and Nagar Haveli ◆ Goa
Maharashtra ◆ Madhya Pradesh
Chattisgarh ◆ Jharkhand

SOUTH AND ISLANDS
Andhra Pradesh ◆ Telangana
Tamil Nadu ◆ Lakshadweep
Puducherry (Pondicherry) ◆ Kerala
Karnataka ◆ Andaman and Nicobar

South Indian food is lighter and largely vegetarian, with some prominent meat-based dishes where religion permits. The states of the south each produce varying degrees of heat in their individual cuisines, and spices are carefully used to moderate body temperature in the intensely hot summers. Pepper, cardamom, and coconut are mainstays, and rice is served generously.

The East will put fish on your plate, as here the river's bounty is evident. People love their rice here, and the area is renowned for its mind-boggling range of sweet treats.

POPULAR INDIAN FOODS

Let's start this journey into regional Indian food with a few popular dishes from across the country. Some you may already know and love, while others will open your eyes (and your taste buds) to something new and beautiful.

RICE AND BREAD

India is one of the top rice producers in the world, and home of the famously fragrant basmati variety. This has led to many creative rice dishes. From lamb biryani to vegetarian lime rice, and many forms in between—like idlis (savory cakes), sweet kheers (puddings), and pohas (flattened rice snacks)—this simple grain is transformed in countless ways throughout the country.

The breadbasket of North India has popularized dishes like rotis and naan. Indians eat homemade breads, both leavened and unleavened, that are prepared in a matter of minutes. Some are served plain, while others are stuffed with vegetables and meats to make a hearty meal by themselves. Rice-based breads are also popular in the southern states.

SNACKS AND LIGHT FARE

If small eats are your thing, this is the right cuisine. India abounds with what I like to call meals-between-meals. There's a wide variety of dosas (fermented crêpes), flatbreads, lip-smacking chaats (roadside savory snacks), and vegetable pakoras. If you're vegetarian or vegan, this part of Indian food is a real delight. Snacks in Indian cuisine are a little treat, usually combining different textures and sweet, salty, hot, and tangy flavors all in one mouthful.

SALADS, CHUTNEYS, AND PICKLES

Indian salads include leafy herbs and fresh vegetables. Curd, lime, and digestive spices are normally part of the dressing.

Chutneys are condiments made with a variety of vegetables, fruits, and spices. In the South, they are predominantly coconut-based, but in other regions they can be tomato- or peanut-based. Chutneys are eaten as side dishes during the main meal, and are usually ground and prepared fresh.

Indian pickles are very different from the brined or vinegar-based pickles of the West. Pickling is a much-loved part of our cuisine, and families pass recipes through generations. Fruits and vegetables are chopped and dried at the peak of summer and left to soak in delightful blends of spices, salt, and oils. Some regions also specialize in pickling meat and fish. Pickles (achaar) are served sparingly in single-serving tablespoons, because they pack quite a punch.

VEGETABLES AND DALS

Indian cuisine is truly a celebration of vegetables. If you ever want to go completely meatless, this is the cuisine with the most variety and flavor. Vegetables are a mainstay in our diet and part of why the cuisine is so balanced. They can be prepared with gravy or dry, and the array is truly mind-boggling.

Dals (lentils) are a staple of the Indian diet. They are served at least a few times a week in most households, and they reflect the diversity of Indian cooking, with flavors that change from home to home and region to region. Dal-chawal, a simple dish of lentils and rice, is considered by many to be the most comforting of all Indian foods.

VEGAN AND ALLIUM-FREE

There are religious communities in India that forbid the use of garlic, onion, and certain root vegetables. In Ayurveda, too, garlic is believed to heat the body and raise anger levels. Many vegetarian dishes can be made allium-free with substitutes like asafetida, a flavoring made from the taproot of a tree indigenous to India, which has a strong, garlicky aroma.

Veganism has long been a part of the Indian diet, so many traditional Indian dishes are already devoid of animal-derived foods.

MEAT AND POULTRY

Delicious things happen to meat and poultry in India. Various spices and cooking styles, such as roasting, braising, frying, steaming, and slow cooking, give us a delicious range of dishes. Meat is often combined with vegetables, rice, and fruit to create fabulous results.

Indian Food and Dietary Restrictions

If you are vegetarian or have dietary restrictions, such as gluten-free, vegan, nut-free, or allium-free, Indian food is perhaps one of the most welcoming and encompassing cuisines in its style and variety. Religious dictates, climate, and topography have all contributed to create healthy, flavorful dishes that naturally fall into these subcategories.

Many of the recipes in this book offer guidelines and tips to address things like sugar-free cooking, or substitutes and modifications for people with special dietary requirements, so that cooking and eating is a joy for all.

Beef and other meats in India are cooked thoroughly, and there is no concept of medium or rare. Cooking is timed for thorough doneness. It is essential to cook meat for as long as the recipe suggests, since the flavors of the spices and masalas are best with well-done meats.

EGGS, FISH, AND SEAFOOD

Even a simple scrambled egg in India, or bhurji as it is popularly called, makes wonderful use of fresh and ground spices. Eggs find their way into curries, stir-fries, and even biryanis.

With the Indian Ocean on one side and the Arabian Sea on the other, India has abundant seafood. Freshwater fish are also common inland from the many rivers scattered throughout the country. Each region has found unique ways of currying, frying, steaming, and grilling fish and crustaceans, in keeping with what grows locally.

DRINKS AND DESSERTS

Sometimes cooling, sometimes fortifying, drinks in India are intricately linked to the climate of the region. Flowers, fruits, dairy, and spices are used, and each region has its own specialties.

Desserts and sweet treats are a joy across the country, and they also hold a special place in religious and cultural festivals. Many sweets are made as offerings to gods, and no celebration, big or small, is complete without them.

FROM THE KITCHEN TO THE TABLE

To get started on your Indian culinary adventure, I suggest stocking up on some indispensable spices and pantry essentials. Most of what you need is available at good Indian, Asian, or Middle Eastern grocery stores in your area, where you'll probably have access to the freshest range of products at good prices. Another great way to shop for the Indian kitchen is online. You will find my recommendations for online sites in the Resources section (page 242). Once you have the basics on hand, cooking Indian food won't seem that complex.

India is still largely an agriculture-based economy. The yearly monsoon makes the land fertile and allows a wide range of vegetables, grains, beans, and legumes to grow. Fruit-growing belts give the world some of the most beloved produce, like the Alphonso mango and the Indian chikoo (sapodilla).

Indian households buy their produce daily or weekly. People prefer to cook with fresh ingredients and rarely use canned or preserved food. Grains and dals are usually purchased in larger quantities and stored in pantries. This is just a practical way of stocking food, since Indian families tend to be large, and dried lentils and grains have a longer shelf life.

When it comes to spices, I recommend buying in small quantities, whether you're stocking your pantry or following a single recipe. It's always best to consume these seasonings rather quickly, and it makes storing them in airtight containers easier, too.

INDIAN PANTRY STAPLES

Indian, Chinese, or Asian grocery stores will stock most of the staples listed here. And you may even find some ingredients in the ethnic foods aisle of your local supermarket. Whatever you don't find locally, you can find online. GroceryBabu.com, iShopIndian.com, and Shop.KhanaPakana.com are among the many online sources for Indian groceries.

Dried Mango Powder

Cane Jaggery

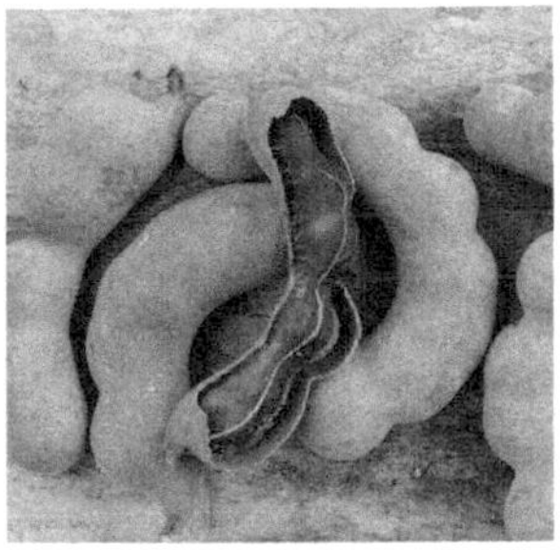

Tamarind Fruit

DRIED RAW MANGO POWDER: Also known as amchur, this yellowish powder is made from sun-dried raw mangoes. It is used as a souring agent in many dishes and has a strong, tart flavor. It is also a tenderizer for meats, and adds a tanginess to some tandoori preparations. The powder is also sprinkled on many snacks and dals, and is added to many salad dressings to provide a sour flavor.

JAGGERY, PALM SUGAR, AND ROCK SUGAR: Unrefined date palm, cane juice, or palm sap is shaped into a solid cone known as jaggery. It is an important part of Indian cooking and is used as a more organic substitute for sugar in many sweet and savory dishes that need to be well balanced. Palm sugar is made from palm tree sap. Rock sugar is hardened sugar crystals.

KOKUM: A member of the mangosteen family, kokum (*Garcinia indica*) is a fruit-based souring agent. In Goa and some other regions, they use it as a substitute for tamarind.

ROCK SALT (KALA NAMAK): Rock salt is used as a natural preservative and a flavor enhancer in savory Indian dishes. It is also known as halite, the mineral form of sodium chloride (NaCl), which comes from salt mountains. It is generally colorless or yellow, but may also be light blue, dark blue, or pink. Rock salt is widely used in Indian food for its therapeutic properties and its taste. It is less salty than regular table salt and is known to cool the body internally, reduce blood pressure, and aid in digestion. You will find it used more often in snacks because of its distinct taste and the way it enhances the flavors of the other spices. Certain religious communities also use it while fasting, since regular salt is forbidden.

TAMARIND PULP AND PASTE: A lot of Indian food is an interplay of sweet, salty, sour, and spicy. Tamarind is a pulpy fruit that is used to add distinct tanginess to many different dishes. Tamarind is sold both as a pulp and as a paste. The paste is simple to use and can be diluted as called for in the recipe. To use tamarind pulp, cover it with water and allow it to soften for several minutes. With your fingers or the back of a spoon, mash the tamarind until it comes apart and colors the water. Strain the mixture to remove the pulp and seeds, and use as directed in the recipe.

VINEGAR: Many dishes that have Portuguese influences use vinegar. Popular vinegars include toddy, coconut, and palm vinegars. If these are unavailable, white vinegar is a close substitute.

Oils and Ghee

While ghee (clarified butter) finds its way into almost every variation of Indian cuisine, it's the kind of oils used that distinguish one region from the other. Each oil has its own distinct flavor, and having a few different oils in your Indian pantry will help you replicate these flavors. In this book, most recipes called for vegetable oil or ghee, and a few call for coconut oil and sesame oil. Be sure to buy these in small quantities, because oils do get rancid over time. Some other types of oil commonly used in Indian food include peanut oil and mustard oil—although you won't need them for the recipes here. Canola oil or unsalted butter are sometimes used as alternatives for ghee, but the taste is different.

Herbs and Aromatics

For Indians, herbs and aromatics such as ginger and garlic are not just flavor makers—they are deeply rooted in our culture and used in medicine as well. While it may seem as though a whole load of flavorings goes into our food, each is used in a dish for its cooling, warming, or therapeutic benefits.

CILANTRO LEAVES (DHANIYA): The leaves and stems of the young coriander plant, also called cilantro, are used as a base in wet masalas and spice mixes, or added at the end of the cooking process for many different dishes. The plant grows across nearly the entire country. When buying cilantro, choose bunches with strong aromas and medium, bright green leaves.

CURRY LEAVES (KADDIPATTA): Curry leaves are used widely in Indian cuisine for their digestive, antioxidant, and therapeutic values, and are added at the start or middle of meal preparations. A popular misconception is that curry leaves taste like curry, the spice blend. This isn't so. Rather, they have a mild, herbal flavor. Fresh curry leaves are preferred, but you can also buy frozen or dried leaves, or freeze extra leaves yourself. If you can't find them, it's best to simply leave them out of the recipe, as there is no substitute.

> Asafetida is a common substitute for onion, garlic, and ginger, as it mimics their aromas to some extent, and is used by religious communities that cannot eat allium.

GARLIC (LEHSUN): Garlic goes wherever ginger does in Indian food—at least, most of the time. The addition of other spices and oils mellows its pungency, so its flavor doesn't shout as much. Look for firm heads with fat, juicy cloves. Young garlic is also excellent in curries.

FRESH GINGER (ADRAK): This root spice is used extensively in Indian cuisine and has a warming effect on the body. When selecting ginger, make sure the skin is intact. If your vendor allows it, snap off a small piece of one of the nodes. It should break easily, with few fibers, and have a pleasant aroma. If the ginger is too fibrous or dry inside, don't buy it.

GREEN CHILES (HARI MIRCHI): Popular throughout the country, these slender green flavor bombs are used in almost all vegetarian and meat-based dishes. A little goes a long way, and some chiles are quite a bit hotter than others. The seeds are more potent than the green flesh, so remove some, if not all, depending on your spice threshold. When buying green chiles, keep in mind that the lighter-colored, longer varieties are less spicy, and the shorter, dark green ones are very hot. Thai and serrano chiles are widely available and are great options for any of the recipes in this book that call for green chiles.

MINT (PUDINA): The leaves of the mint plant are used as a garnish in Indian cooking, and in curd-based salads, relishes, and drinks, too. Mint is used for its cooling properties and is prominent in the North. When selecting mint, look for fresh green leaves with a strong aroma.

ONIONS (PYAAZ): Onions are the base for hundreds of dishes in Indian cuisine. They form the texture and flavor for stocks, marinades, and curries. Indian onions are red skinned and sharper in taste than Spanish or white onions. When a recipe calls for onions in this book, I mean red onions. Yellow onions won't brown the way red onions are required to in Indian food and may turn sweeter when browned. You can substitute white onions, but do not cook them past the browning point.

Dry Spices

Spices grow abundantly in the hot and humid southern states of India, and are some of the finest in the world. Remember that spices are half flavor and half aroma; their enemies are air and dampness. It's wise to buy small quantities of dry spices and grind them as you need them, or if you must, buy very small quantities of ground spices. Store the leftover ground spices in nonreactive stainless steel tins or in glass containers in a cool, dry place or, even better, in the refrigerator. Remember that ground spices don't last as long as whole spices, so use them as quickly as possible.

To grind whole spices, you will need an electric spice grinder or an extra coffee grinder used solely for grinding spices. A mortar and pestle also works well, but you're better off using this method only if the spices are roasted and cooled first, to make it easier to grind them by hand.

ASAFETIDA (HING): Asafetida is the dried gum oleoresin exuded from the living rhizome or taproot of a specific tree native to India. It has a fetid aroma, but when tempered in oil, imparts a flavor similar to onion and garlic. It is also used medicinally to treat digestive issues.

BLACK PEPPER (KAALI MIRI): Kerala is known for producing the finest peppercorns in the world. Pepper lends itself whole or ground to the wide varieties of garam masala, an essential Indian spice blend made throughout the country.

CARAWAY SEEDS (SHAHI JEERA): This is another spice confused in the looks department with cumin, though it tastes nothing like it. Caraway has wonderful digestive properties and is also used in spice blends. It has a sharp taste that sweetens as you chew it. This is one of those spices that is good to chew just on its own after a heavy meal.

Asafetida Cakes

Caraway Seeds

Cardamom Pods

CARDAMOM (ELAICHI): Mellow and sweet in flavor, cardamom imparts the most wonderful aroma in both savory and sweet dishes. It is grown extensively in the south of the country. There are two types of cardamom—green and black. The green variety has a more mellow, sweet flavor, and the black variety is bigger, more robust, and pungent. Black cardamom is used sparingly, as it tends to overpower dishes. Cardamom grows in seed-filled pods, and you can buy it still in the pods or as seeds only. In this book, I will specify when seeds are needed; otherwise, I mean pods.

CAROM SEEDS (AJWAIN): These small seeds have a flavor reminiscent of thyme. They are widely used as a digestive aid and are often chewed plain to relieve stomachache and heartburn. They are used sparingly in cooking to add a mild but notable flavor to dishes. You can find carom seeds online, but in a pinch, dried thyme, cumin, and caraway seeds are often used as substitutes.

CHAAT MASALA: This tangy and mildly hot spice blend can be purchased ready-made or you can make it at home. It has a range of ingredients, including dried raw mango powder, ground cumin, and pepper. It is widely used on Indian snacks and in cooking. Buy small quantities, and store it in an airtight container in the fridge. Some masalas, such as garam masala, are best when they are homemade and more fragrant—so I have provided recipes for them in chapter 2 (pages 44 and 45).

Cloves

Coriander Seeds

Fennel Seeds

What is sold in the West as curry powder is actually a blend of spices. But in India, there is no such thing as a one-size-fits-all curry powder. Different recipes use blends of spices in various proportions to create unique spice blends, called masalas. Depending on the recipe, masalas or spice blends can be wet or dry. You will see how easy it is to make these by yourself, instead of buying ready-made curry mixes.

CINNAMON (DALCHINI): This fragrant, woody spice is essential to a lot of Indian food. Cassia cinnamon is the type used in Indian cooking, as it is sweeter and has a slightly mellower fragrance than Sri Lankan cinnamon sticks. It is used in both sweet and savory dishes.

CLOVES (LAVANG): This spice is used in curries, chai mixes, and a host of savory dishes throughout India. It is also known for its medicinal properties and is a great remedy for a toothache.

CORIANDER SEEDS (AKKA DHANIYA): These have a nutty, lemony flavor and are used in various spice blends. They are usually used in powdered form, sometimes roasted before grinding. Roasting imparts a very different flavor to this seed and makes it more intense and earthy. Ground coriander is simply the powdered version of the seed, and is widely used in Indian cooking as well.

CUMIN SEEDS (JEERA): Cumin is a well-known digestive aid. It balances the heat in a dish and cools the digestive tract. These thin, tiny seeds are used as a tempering spice, roasted and ground as a garnish, or added to cooling

Fenugreek

Indian Bay Leaf

Mustard Seeds

drinks. The seeds have an earthy, nutty flavor. Good cumin will have a nice aroma. Ground cumin is simply the powdered version of the cumin seed, and can be made from raw or roasted seeds for slightly different flavor profiles.

DRIED RED CHILES (SOOKHI LAAL MIRCH): Dried red chiles are often used in Indian cuisine. You'll see recipes that call for Kashmiri chiles or Bydagi chiles or others. Each has varying degrees of heat, but all add that beautiful red hue to Indian food. Buy small quantities and store them in dry, airtight containers.

FENNEL SEEDS (SAUNF): These tiny crescent seeds have amazing digestive properties and a licorice-like flavor. Fennel is used in a number of spice blends and is frequently enjoyed with rock sugar after meals, to aid in digestion.

FENUGREEK (METHI): Fenugreek seeds are small, angular, brownish seeds, which have a pleasantly bitter flavor and strong aroma. They are used sparingly and are often toasted to enhance their pungent aroma. They are then ground, alone or with other spices. Fenugreek is a common ingredient in curry and pickle blends. It is also used to temper various vegetable and dal dishes to enhance the aroma and taste.

INDIAN BAY LEAF (TEJPATTA): This is in the same family as the bay laurel, but the aroma and flavor are more similar to Indian cinnamon. The leaves of Indian bay are more leathery, longer, and browner than Mediterranean bay leaves. They are not meant to be eaten with the meal but merely to flavor the food at the start of the cooking process. Remove the leaves and discard them from the dish before eating. Indian bay leaves can be found at Indian and Pakistani specialty grocers. However, if you can't find them, standard Mediterranean variety bay leaves can be used. The taste difference is very subtle.

MUSTARD SEEDS (RAI): These tiny seeds are used at the start of cooking a dish to flavor the oil. They add crunch and a slightly bitter taste to the dish. When buying, look for whole black mustard seeds.

NIGELLA (KALONJI): These tiny seeds are known for their strong therapeutic value. They have a nutty flavor and are used in many tempering oils to add crunch. Because of their rich black color, they are often used as a decorative spice on breads and biscuits. These are also widely used in Indian pickles and to make a popular spice blend, paanch phoran.

Not to be confused with a curry blend, garam masala (which literally means "warm spice blend") adds depth of flavor to a dish and warmth to the body. It is usually (but not always) added toward the end of the dish in small quantities. It uses whole spices in various proportions, sometimes roasted before grinding and sometimes not. There are various types of garam masalas from various regions; I recommend making your own (see pages 44 and 45) so that the fragrance and flavors are more authentic.

NUTMEG (JAIPHAL): Nutmeg is a strong spice with a wonderful aroma. On a single fruit, you get nutmeg inside and mace, another spice, covering it outside. Nutmeg has medicinal properties. Because it is poisonous in large quantities, however, it is grated sparingly into dishes and spice blends.

RED CHILI POWDER (LAAL MIRCH POWDER): This is an indispensable ingredient in the Indian kitchen. Chili powders in India are made from a mix of various types of dried chiles grown in the country, and the different blends play a large role in the heat and color of the dishes in which they are used. Kashmiri chili powder imparts a lot of bright color and not too much heat. Deghi mirch powder is a much hotter chili powder that also contributes a bright color to foods.

Nigella

Saffron

Turmeric

Depending on the brand of store-bought chili powder, the labels may or may not mention the type of chiles used. The best thing to do is to look for the generic Indian name for chili powder—laal mirch—at an Indian grocer or online. Because these types of chili powder are notable for their strong color, a simple substitute can be equal amounts of cayenne pepper and paprika. However, because this is such an important element of Indian cuisine, I strongly recommend sourcing laal mirch powder for the most authentic flavor and color.

SAFFRON (KESAR): This is one of the costliest spices by weight on the planet. It is the stigma of the crocus flower. It is used sparingly to impart its characteristic, golden yellow hue and distinct fragrance to sweet and savory dishes. Buy small quantities and store the threads in a cool dry place, preferably in a glass container.

TURMERIC (HALDI): In its fresh form, turmeric looks a lot like gingerroot, and, like ginger, it is also dried and ground into a powder used commonly in Indian cuisine. Turmeric is an indispensable spice in the Indian pantry, prized for its rich yellow-orange color and antiseptic and anti-inflammatory properties. It is typically used sparingly in the beginning of the cooking process.

Spices need dark and very dry storage conditions. Use nonreactive containers to store masalas, especially the ground spices. Stainless steel is the best, followed by glass.

Legumes and Beans (Dals)

Dals are an essential part of Indian cuisine and are eaten frequently in every home. They are simple, protein-rich, and easy to digest. "Dal" refers to dozens of varieties of dried split peas, beans, lentils, and other kinds of beanlike seeds that are collectively called pulses. In India we typically say "lentil" when we mean dal, which encompasses so much more than just lentils.

"Dal" can also refer to the spicy or aromatic side dishes that are made with dals and a wide variety of other ingredients. Cooked dals are a staple across homes in India, and are made at least twice a week. They are a vital source of protein for the strictly vegetarian or vegan and a powerhouse of health and nutrition. The sheer number of recipes and combinations is mind-boggling, and every region and home has its own beautiful range of preparations.

Dals are usually bought dehydrated and then soaked for a few hours before cooking. The general rule is that split, skinned lentils benefit from at least 3 hours of soaking if cooked on a stovetop, or no soaking at all if cooked in a pressure cooker. Beans need to be soaked for at least 4 hours to overnight and cooked until tender, which could be anywhere from 1 to 2 hours on a stovetop. In a pressure cooker, cooking time is reduced by half.

If you plan to make Indian food often, here are some dals to stock up on. Just remember to store them in airtight glass or plastic containers in a dry location.

BLACK LENTILS (URAD DAL): There are two types of black lentils used in Indian cooking: whole lentils, which are black, and split lentils, which are known as white urad dal. The whole lentils have a strong flavor, while the split lentils are skinned, resulting in a creamier and less pronounced flavor. Also called black gram, these black lentils are sticky, and therefore they are commonly used in recipes as a binding agent. They are also used to flavor cooking oil, due to their inherently nutty taste.

CHICKPEAS: Two types of chickpeas (also known as garbanzo beans) are found in India: a smaller, dark-skinned bean known as kaala channa (black chickpea), and a larger, white-skinned bean known as kabuli channa (white chickpea). Delicious, wholesome dishes are made with both. Chickpeas are usually purchased dry and soaked overnight to plump them up before using. Chickpeas also come in two forms: whole or split. Split yellow chickpeas are known as channa dal or Bengal gram. Whole chickpeas are called chole or kabuli channa.

MUNG BEANS (MOONG DAL): Mung beans are sold both whole and skinned. The whole version is green and can be sprouted or cooked as is. The dal, made from skinned and split beans, is bright yellow. It has a lovely, mellow flavor and is one of the easiest-to-digest dals, often given to babies in a mash-up with rice as a comforting, nutritious meal.

PIGEON PEAS (TUVAR DAL): These are important legumes across India, especially in Gujarat. They are split and skinned in their young form, and as whole peas they are made into a dry vegetable dish. They have a distinct, nutty flavor.

RED LENTILS (MASOOR DAL): These lentils are brown on the outside and deep orange on the inside. Masoor dal has an earthy flavor and is very popular in North India. It is commonly used to make lentil soups.

Grains and Flours

Rice and flours of many types are common in Indian cuisine and make it a well-balanced diet. Some of the common ones found in the Indian kitchen are given next. For general measurements, flours should be bought in ½-pound to 2-pound units (depending on your rate of use) and stored in a cool, dry place in airtight containers and jars. While some of these grains and flours can be found in any typical grocery store, many will have to be sourced from an Indian grocery store or from an online vendor.

The grains and flours listed here are all used in this book. Some other flours that are common in Indian cooking include finger millet flour (nachni), pearl millet flour (bajra), sorghum or white millet flour (jowar), and soy flour. Check what flours and grains you need for a specific recipe. Leftover flours will keep well in airtight containers in the refrigerator.

CHICKPEA FLOUR (BESAN): This is used to make a range of snacks and sweets, such as pakoras (fritters), sweet ladoos (sweet balls), khandvi (savory snack rolls), dhoklas (vegetarian snacks), and other nibbles. This is a good gluten-free flour, which is why it is often stocked in natural foods stores. Chickpea flour has a distinctive taste, so if you substitute something else, the flavor will be quite different. If you can't find it locally, order it online.

CORNMEAL AND CORNSTARCH (MAKKI KA ATTA AND MAKAI KA ATTA): Cornmeal is made from dried corn and is yellow, and cornstarch is made from the starch of the corn kernels and is white. Cornmeal is used to make the popular makki ka roti (flatbread) from Punjab.

MILLET: Indian cuisine uses many varieties of whole millet, including Foxtail, Barnyard, pearl, and Kodo. They come in shades of yellow, red, gray, and white; add a nice, nutty flavor to a dish; and are a fabulous source of nutrition. You can substitute rice for most of them. Millet is great for the gluten-free diet, and is also popular in the drier regions of India, since it needs very little water to grow.

RICE (CHAWAL): Indian food uses a good deal of rice. Buy 2-pound packages for single or double servings, or bulk up with larger quantities if you're feeding a large family. Store rice in an airtight glass, plastic, or stainless steel container, or, alternatively, in the burlap bag it may come packed in. If you don't use rice regularly, it is okay to keep it stored this way for six months to one year, as aged rice tastes even better. However, it is important to keep it away from moisture and wash your rice thoroughly before cooking. Basmati rice is a wonderful, aromatic rice that goes well with all types of Indian meals.

RICE FLOUR (CHAWAL KA ATTA): This is used to make a number of breads, and as a thickening agent in many dishes. This, too, is a good gluten-free option.

SEMOLINA (RAVA): This coarse, purified wheat middling is used in a wide range of dishes, both sweet and savory, from crispy dosas to comforting sweet porridges. If you can't find Indian-style rava, semolina flour will work well in its place.

WHEAT FLOUR, WHOLE AND REFINED (GEHUN KA ATTA AUR MAIDA): Whole-wheat flour is essential in the Indian kitchen and is used to make breads and certain sweets. Refined (all-purpose) flour is also used in a number of breads. Buy small quantities, 1 or 2 pounds, so that it is used quickly. Store any leftovers in an airtight container in a cool, dark place.

Proteins

Dairy products are a huge part of the Indian diet—especially for those who are vegetarian. Yogurt and various types of milk solids find their way into delicious dishes. Paneer is a fresh, unripened cheese that is pressed until firm, similar to farmer's cheese or pot cheese. If you can't find it, try drained ricotta, unsalted drained small-curd cottage cheese, or halloumi cheese.

Chicken, mutton, goat, pork, and beef are common animal proteins, though beef and pork are taboo in some religions. Fish and crustaceans are widely eaten in the coastal areas, and freshwater fish is loved by communities mainly in the East.

ESSENTIAL EQUIPMENT

The modern Indian kitchen is incomplete without a few basic tools and appliances. Invest in the following items to make your culinary journey a no-fuss, enjoyable process.

SPICE GRINDER: An electric spice grinder or a coffee grinder is a very handy tool in the Indian kitchen. Back home we have mixer-grinders that do the job of wet as well as dry grinding. If you're using a coffee grinder for your spices, make sure you keep separate ones for grinding coffee and spices. Alternatively, you could use a high-powered blender.

MORTAR AND PESTLE: A little pounding goes a long way in releasing aromatics in the Indian kitchen, and a mortar and pestle is indispensable for that, as well as for grinding roasted spices for seasoning blends.

ROLLING BOARD AND PINS: These are necessary to shape flatbreads.

A KADHAI AND OTHER POTS AND PANS: Also known as an Indian wok, the traditional kadhai is a bowl-shaped cast-iron cooking vessel with two handles. Nowadays you can find kadhais that are made with different materials, including steel, copper cores (for better heat conduction), anodized aluminum, and nonstick versions. They come with both flat and round bases, with and without lids, and in various sizes.

If you can't get your hands on a traditional Indian kadhai, you can use a larger, heavy-bottomed saucepan, frying pan, or skillet, with or without a lid. Invest in at least one cast-iron skillet, griddle, or traditional Indian tava (a large flat pan with a concave center) to roast spices and cook flatbreads.

Kadhais are an indispensable part of the Indian kitchen, and many dishes can be cooked in them, similar to the way a wok is used in a Chinese kitchen. In some parts of the country, an inverted kadhai is placed over a flame, and thin Indian breads (roomali roti) are cooked over this rounded surface. Kadhais are also sometimes used as stove-to-table serving bowls, with more ornate ones sold exclusively for serving.

SPOONS: A few wooden and stainless steel spoons are handy. You need non-reactive utensils like these when cooking with a lot of spices and condiments.

NICE TO HAVE

INDIAN SPICE BOX (MASALA DABBA): These round, stainless steel boxes have six or seven circular open bowls inside that keep all your spices, either whole or ground, in perfect condition for longer. Stainless steel is nonreactive and keeps spices cool and in a dark environment.

ELECTRIC SLOW COOKER: Although it's not essential, this is a handy appliance for Indian home cooking. Many of the recipes in this book can be prepared using a slow cooker; just look for the "Make It Easier" tip at the end for instructions on how to convert the recipe for slow cooking.

PRESSURE COOKER: Lentil soups, curries made with pork, beef, and mutton, and even some pilafs are perfect candidates for the pressure cooker. Follow along with my handy pressure cooker tips if you own one. In this book, the timings and special tips are for my electric Instant Pot 7-in-1 pressure cooker. Because every pressure cooker is different, be sure to read Appendix A (page 237), which explains how to convert my pressure cooker tips for your cooker. It also has handy tips for cooking dals and beans.

Cooking Dals in a Slow Cooker

Lentils and beans can also benefit from slow cooking; it makes the lentils creamier and beans fluffier, and it allows the spices to blend wonderfully. You will create the flavorings and masala pastes first, add them to the uncooked dals, and then cook everything together in the slow cooker until tender.

For lentils, I use one and a half times more water than lentils in the slow cooker. Cook them for 3 hours on High or 6 to 8 hours on Low. For a lentil-bean combination, the cooking time can be increased to 8 to 9 hours on Low.

If this is your first time cooking lentils, or if you're cooking an unfamiliar kind of lentil, begin checking the lentils after 5 hours (if cooking on Low), and then every 30 minutes until they are tender.

For beans, I like to presoak them overnight to remove any harmful residues and cut their cooking time. Discard the soaking water the next day. I typically cook beans for 6 to 7 hours on Low. This time is for beans that have been soaked overnight. The water or liquid in the slow cooker should cover the beans by about 2 inches.

If this is your first time cooking beans, or if you're cooking an unfamiliar kind of bean, begin checking the beans after 5 hours, and then every 30 minutes until they are tender.

TIPS AND TRICKS FOR MAKING INDIAN COOKING EASIER

Cooking Indian food doesn't need to be complicated or time consuming. Here are a few things to keep in mind before you start your Indian culinary adventure.

PERFECT PREP

Good mise en place is important. *Mise en place* is a French culinary term that literally means "putting in place." It refers to getting all the ingredients you will need on hand, measured, and prepped before you start cooking. Many people are overwhelmed by the number of ingredients and steps involved in cooking Indian food. There is a simple solution to that. Get all the ingredients measured and prepped (chopped, blended, ground) before you do the actual cooking. When everything is in front of you, you will find that the assembly is actually pretty simple.

SAUTÉING ONIONS AND MAKING MASALA BASES IN OIL

The key to a good curry is the sautéing at the initial stage. Most recipes will call for you to sauté onions—or onions and then tomatoes—and the spice paste. I have seen many cooks sauté onions quite lightly or just until they are translucent; this will not give you the desired depth of flavor or the consistency of an Indian curry. Unless the recipe specifically says you should sauté the onion just until it's softened, you must take the onions further and brown them quite fearlessly. The trick is to prevent burning by moderating the heat, and, more important, adding a few drops of water to reduce the temperature in the pan. What water also does is soften the onions, so you're left with browned and cooked onions that are a good base for most curries. Do the same with tomatoes; sauté them until they are mushy and totally incorporated into the oil.

WASHING RICE AND LENTILS

Rice is always washed before cooking. The separateness of rice grains is a point of pride in Indian cuisine, and washing rice removes extra starchiness and residues that might make the grains stick to one another during cooking. An easy way to wash your rice is to place it in a bowl and fill the bowl with water. Run your fingers through the rice and water, then pour out the water through a fine-mesh strainer. Repeat the process about three times, until the water gets a little less cloudy. Follow the same procedure to remove any residues from beans and lentils.

Here are a few more shortcuts, tips, and tricks, from my kitchen to yours, to make cooking Indian food fun and easy.

- When cooking in a slow cooker, a little prep goes a long way. Where recipes allow for it, blend spices, wet and dry, to a fine paste and then add the mixture to the cooker. This not only enhances flavor but also reduces grittiness and the risk of a raw aftertaste.

Adding the Tadka Flourish

Tadka is a technique of adding flavor to a dish by using a heated oil that is infused with spices and herbs. Loosely, a tadka can be likened to tempering—a way of transferring the flavors of spices, lentils, and herbs to the food in a final flourish. The term *tadka* is used interchangeably to refer to the technique, the resulting flavored oil, and the ingredients that will go into the oil.

Tadkas are never made in advance. They are made fresh, when the dish is prepared and waiting for its garnish. I personally love the way the spices and herbs crackle and spit in the hot oil, and how they transform and lift the flavors of a dish as they are added to it. Sometimes a tadka oil will be flavored at the start of the cooking process, before the other ingredients are added. In these cases, it will be clearly described in the recipe method.

Not all dishes need a tadka, but the ones that have them are greatly enhanced in flavor and aroma. I feel it acts as a reminder of some of the ingredients that may have gone into the dish at the beginning of the cooking process. Tadkas sometimes serve as balancing elements as well, making all the ingredients in a dish work more harmoniously together.

- Canned chickpeas (garbanzo beans) can be substituted for dried ones. This saves you the hassle of soaking them overnight and cuts cooking time, too. Just remember to add the precooked beans toward the end of the cooking process, when the spice mixture is cooked through.
- Try this simple make-ahead curry base to reduce prep time: Chop 3 medium onions, 3 medium tomatoes, and 2 green chiles, and prepare 1 tablespoon Ginger-Garlic Paste (page 46). Heat 2 tablespoons vegetable oil over medium-high heat and sauté the onions until brown. Add the tomatoes and sauté until mushy. Add the green chiles and ginger-garlic paste and sauté until the rawness disappears. Freeze 1 to 2 ladles of this mixture in small containers for up to a month. To use, pop one serving of curry base into a pan for the dish you are making.

- To make onions brown faster and more evenly, add a pinch of salt or sugar. You can also sauté more than the recipe requires and refrigerate the extra browned onions for up to 2 weeks.
- Combine ½ cup each of garlic and ginger in a spice grinder, along with 1 seeded green chile, and process until smooth, then transfer the mixture to an airtight glass container. This handy spice mixture is used in almost all savory Indian dishes, and it keeps for weeks in the refrigerator.

TIME TO EAT

Indian food is traditionally served in metal bowls placed on a metal platter, or thali. The bowls contain the various courses, all represented on one plate—tiny appetizers, rice and bread courses, meats, vegetables, pickles, and even dessert.

Another traditional way of serving Indian food is on a banana leaf. It follows the same plating principles of the thali but is considered healthier to eat from and is also biodegradable. Modern homes also serve Indian food in ethnic or contemporary bowls and serving platters and allow guests and family members to help themselves.

> Indian food is best eaten with one's hand—more specifically, with the right hand. The left hand is considered unclean, and while nobody will voice displeasure, try eating with your right hand even if you are left-handed.

Drinks can be served in clay tumblers or steel glasses for that Indian feel. Table accents like marigolds, clay lamps, and rose petals strewn around the dishes make for a pretty Indian setting when entertaining.

While Indian food is traditionally eaten by hand, guests must always be given an option to use cutlery if they are more comfortable that way. In Indian culture, there is a saying, "Athithi deo bhava," which means, "The guest is akin to God." His or her needs are always the highest priority.

Icons and Recipe Labels

In this book you will see labels and icons attached to each recipe that indicate the recipe's regional origin, spice level, and dietary properties.

SOUTH INDIA

The map icon with each dish explains the origin of the dish in India—specifically which region this recipe hails from, South, North, East, or West and Central India.

I have also included Indian-Chinese recipes that are very popular in mainstream Indian cuisine and prepared almost everywhere in the country. These will be indicated with an Indian-Chinese icon.

Anglo-Indian recipes have an icon as well. These are dishes made popular during British rule in India, when Western dishes and cooking techniques were given an Indian twist. These dishes are my own family recipes that I hope you enjoy.

The peppers 🌶🌶🌶 will let you know how hot a recipe is if you prepare it as written. Of course, you can always adjust the heat by adding more or less of the hot spices. No peppers means not a bit of heat, one pepper means mild, two peppers means medium, and three peppers is a hot dish.

FESTIVAL FOOD means this dish is served at Indian festivals and celebrations. The recipe introduction will tell you more.

Dietary labels with the recipes will tell you if a dish is **VEGETARIAN**, **VEGAN**, **EGG-FREE**, **DAIRY-FREE**, **GLUTEN-FREE**, **PEANUT-FREE**, **SOY-FREE**, or **ALLIUM-FREE**. In this book, vegetarian means no meat, poultry, fish, or seafood, but the dish contains eggs or dairy. Vegan means no animal products of any kind.

Wherever possible, you will also see a ***Substitution Tip*** at the bottom of the recipe that makes the recipe suitable for other kinds of dietary restrictions, such as substituting tofu for paneer (an Indian cheese).

2

INDIAN SPICE BLENDS AND HOME REMEDIES

ROASTED CUMIN POWDER

Bhuna Hua Jeera Powder

ALL INDIA

VEGAN
GLUTEN-FREE
PEANUT-FREE
SOY-FREE
ALLIUM-FREE

MAKES ¾ CUP ◆ PREP TIME: 10 MINUTES ◆ COOK TIME: 2 MINUTES

This versatile ingredient can be sprinkled over yogurt or vegetable-based salads, added to dals as a garnish, or incorporated in a variety of dishes. Cumin is a healing spice—its uses range from easing menstrual cramps to curing indigestion. I make small quantities of this powder and use it as quickly as I can, since the lovely aroma diminishes quickly over time.

3½ ounces cumin seeds

1 Heat a cast-iron skillet or tava over high heat. Spread the cumin seeds as evenly as possible on the skillet.

2 Immediately turn the heat to low and stir the cumin seeds to prevent scorching. Continue stirring for 20 to 30 seconds, until the color changes and a strong aroma emanates. Watch out for the cumin becoming too brown. It should only slightly change color and give off a pleasant aroma.

3 Turn off the heat and immediately transfer the roasted cumin to a plate to cool. Spread out in a thin layer.

4 When completely cool, grind the cumin seeds to a fine powder using a dry spice grinder or mortar and pestle.

5 Use immediately and store the remainder for up to 10 days in a glass or stainless steel container with an airtight lid.

Cooking Tip: To test the skillet for readiness, hold your flat palm a few inches above it. When you can feel the heat emanating from the skillet, it is ready for dry roasting.

CORIANDER-CUMIN SPICE BLEND

Dhania Jeera Masala

ALL INDIA

VEGAN
GLUTEN-FREE
PEANUT-FREE
SOY-FREE
ALLIUM-FREE

MAKES ABOUT ¾ CUP ♦ PREP TIME: 15 MINUTES ♦ COOK TIME: 2 MINUTES

This simple spice blend is a handy addition to your spice rack. I like to make small quantities as I need it, because the aroma of this blend is half its flavor. It is used across many recipes and imparts an earthy, wholesome flavor, besides having digestive properties.

½ cup coriander seeds
¼ cup cumin seeds
1½ teaspoons black peppercorns
3 whole cloves
1 (½-inch) cinnamon stick

1 On a plate, place the coriander, cumin, pepper, cloves, and cinnamon. If possible, place the plate in the sun for a few hours.

2 Heat a cast-iron skillet or tava over medium heat and add the spice mixture. Turn the heat to low so as not to burn the spices. Keep stirring at intervals to turn the spices. In 2 minutes, you should be able to smell the aromas of the spice. Turn the heat off.

3 Transfer the spice blend to a plate to cool completely. Blend in a mortar and pestle or spice grinder and store immediately in an airtight jar.

Substitution Tip: You can make this blend with just cumin and coriander, omitting the other spices.

BASIC HOMEMADE GARAM MASALA

ALL INDIA

VEGAN
GLUTEN-FREE
PEANUT-FREE
SOY-FREE
ALLIUM-FREE

MAKES ½ TO ⅔ CUP • PREP TIME: 5 MINUTES • COOK TIME: 20 MINUTES

Garam masala *is literally translated as "warm spice blend," and the spices do just that: they warm the body and have immense therapeutic and medicinal value. While each state and community in India has its own variation, you can safely use this recipe when no specific garam masala is mentioned in a recipe.*

- ¾ tablespoon whole cloves
- 2 tablespoons crushed cinnamon sticks
- 3½ tablespoons cumin seeds
- 1 tablespoon green cardamom pods
- 3 tablespoons peppercorns
- 3½ tablespoons coriander seeds
- 2 tablespoons fennel seeds
- 10 Indian bay leaves or Mediterranean bay leaves
- 3 black cardamom pods

1 Heat a skillet or tava over low heat. Dry roast each of the spices separately except the black cardamom. Keep stirring so that the spices do not burn. As soon as you get a nice aroma from each spice, transfer to a plate and cool.

2 When all the spices completely cool, transfer to a mortar and pestle or spice grinder and grind until totally smooth.

3 Store this aromatic mixture immediately in an airtight jar in a cool, dry place.

Cooking Tip: Instead of dry roasting them on a skillet, you can sun-dry the spices by spreading them on a plate and leaving them in direct sun for at least a whole day.

PUNJABI GARAM MASALA

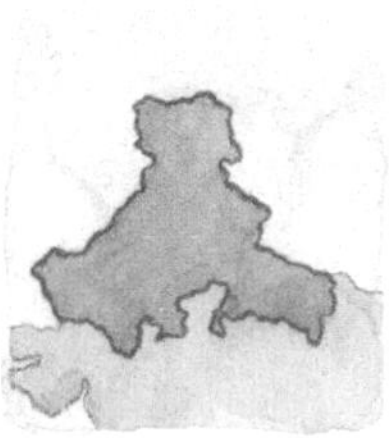

NORTH INDIA

VEGAN
GLUTEN-FREE
PEANUT-FREE
SOY-FREE
ALLIUM-FREE

MAKES 1 CUP ♦ PREP TIME: 15 MINUTES, PLUS 1 DAY TO DRY *This garam masala recipe is commonly used in North Indian dishes like Punjabi Chickpea Curry (page 152), Potato and Tomato Curry (page 127), and Stuffed Bell Peppers (page 134). In general, garam masalas are strong, aromatic spice blends that are incorporated sparingly as an add-on to the main spice blend in a particular recipe.*

1 (1-inch) piece fresh ginger
10 (2-inch) cinnamon sticks
1 whole nutmeg
2 tablespoons whole cloves
½ cup coriander seeds
¼ cup cumin seeds
20 whole green cardamom pods
5 whole black cardamom pods
1½ tablespoons peppercorns
10 Indian bay leaves or Mediterranean bay leaves

1 Spread all the spices on a plate, and place them in the sun for at least a day to dry out and crisp up. Bring inside at night.

2 Using a mortar and pestle or spice grinder, process the ginger first. Next, add the cinnamon, nutmeg, and cloves. Add the coriander, cumin, green and black cardamom, peppercorns, and bay leaves and grind until very fine. If necessary, grind the spices in batches. Mix any batches back together thoroughly.

3 Store immediately in an airtight container in the refrigerator or in a cool, dark place.

Cooking Tip: Once you've used most of the garam masala, transfer the contents to a smaller jar to reduce contact with air and moisture and keep the blend fresh and aromatic.

GINGER-GARLIC PASTE

Adrak-Lehsun Masala

ALL INDIA

VEGAN
GLUTEN-FREE
PEANUT-FREE
SOY-FREE

MAKES 1 CUP ◆ PREP TIME: 15 MINUTES *Ginger-garlic paste is used widely in Indian food, from curries and dry vegetarian dishes to dals and marinades. This is my personal recipe, in which I use a slightly higher ratio of garlic to ginger. I find that while garlic mellows out during the cooking process, ginger tends to shout a bit and may become overpowering.*

1 cup peeled garlic cloves
¾ cup peeled and chopped ginger
2 green chiles (optional)
2 tablespoons chopped cilantro leaves and stems (optional)
Water, for mixing (optional)

1 Using a spice grinder or mortar and pestle, add the garlic, ginger, chiles (if using), and cilantro (if using) and blend until smooth.

2 Add a couple of teaspoons of water if the mixture is too dry and tough to blend. (But don't overdo the water, as it greatly diminishes the shelf life of the paste.) You should end up with a smooth, thick paste.

3 Transfer to a glass container with an airtight lid and store in the refrigerator, where it will keep fresh for about 4 weeks.

Ingredient Tip: You can also add ½ teaspoon turmeric powder, 1 tablespoon oil, or both, while blending, to give the paste a bright yellow hue.

SIMPLE MOUTH FRESHENER

Sada Mukhuvas

WEST AND CENTRAL INDIA

VEGAN
GLUTEN-FREE
PEANUT-FREE
SOY-FREE
ALLIUM-FREE

MAKES ABOUT 1 CUP ♦ PREP TIME: 30 MINUTES ♦ COOK TIME: 20 MINUTES

In India, mouth fresheners—or crunchy mixes of seeds and mild seasonings—are served after meals to cleanse the palate and aid in digestion. This one comes from Gujarat in West India, and it is designed to help ease stomach acidity and make you feel light after a heavy dinner.

Juice of ½ lemon
½ cup fennel seeds
1 tablespoon coriander seeds
3 tablespoons sesame seeds
2 tablespoons carom seeds (optional)
2 tablespoons dill seeds (optional)
1 tablespoon dried coconut slivers
½ teaspoon powdered sugar (optional)
Kosher salt

1 In a small bowl, mix the lemon juice and fennel seeds. Set aside for 10 minutes.

2 Heat a cast-iron skillet or tava over medium-high heat, turn the flame to low, and separately roast the coriander, sesame, carom (if using), and dill seeds (if using) until crisp, stirring continuously and taking care not to burn the seeds, as they are very delicate. Look for a pleasant aroma and crispness in the seeds. Transfer all the seeds to one plate and spread out to cool.

3 In the same hot skillet or tava, add the coconut slivers and roast until light brown, stirring continuously. Transfer to a plate to cool. continued ▶

4 Add the fennel seeds to the skillet, stirring continuously until they are crisp. Transfer to a plate and cool.

5 Mix all the roasted ingredients on a deep plate. Add the sugar (if using) and season with salt. Stir to combine and store in an airtight container for at least 2 to 3 weeks.

Make It Healthier: You can also add 1 tablespoon each sunflower seeds and melon seeds to up the nutritional value. Simply roast them separately and add them into the mix when it is cool.

Serving Tip: Traditionally, mukhwas is served after the meal in a bowl or wooden box with a spoon in it. Remember to use the teaspoon, but do not touch it to your lips. It is considered unhealthy to put one's saliva on a serving spoon.

TURMERIC MILK WITH HONEY

Haldi Doodh

ALL INDIA

VEGETARIAN
EGG-FREE
GLUTEN-FREE
PEANUT-FREE
SOY-FREE
ALLIUM-FREE

SERVES 1 • PREP TIME: 10 MINUTES • COOK TIME: 5 MINUTES *When you have a sore throat that leaves you croaking and in annoying pain, this is just what you need. It is quick to make and instantly calming. Turmeric is renowned for its antiseptic properties and, when combined with honey, another throat soother, the resulting drink is very effective.*

1 cup whole milk
1 (½-inch) piece ginger, grated (optional)
½ teaspoon turmeric powder
1 teaspoon honey

1 In a saucepan, add the milk and ginger (if using), and bring to a gentle boil. Add the turmeric, stir, and turn off the heat.

2 Pour into a mug and add the honey. Stir well and serve.

Cooking Tip: You can heat the milk and ginger in a mug in the microwave for 2 minutes for a quicker drink. Carefully remove the mug and add the turmeric and honey.

Ingredient Tip: The ingredients for home remedies are usually abundantly available in an Indian pantry and have tremendous medicinal value. Most of these kitchen remedies are mild and have no side effects.

PEPPER DECOCTION FOR COUGH AND COLD

Miryaso Kasai

SOUTH INDIA

VEGAN
GLUTEN-FREE
PEANUT-FREE
SOY-FREE
ALLIUM-FREE

SERVES 1 ◆ PREP TIME: 5 MINUTES ◆ COOK TIME: 15 MINUTES *Black pepper has been used for centuries to treat respiratory conditions and reduce inflammation in the body. And ginger (fresh or dried), rock sugar, and holy basil (a variety native to India) are also popular for their antiseptic, expectorant, and restorative properties. This decoction is fairly strong, so you can dilute it by adding a small amount of milk. I find it has immediate benefits.*

1½ teaspoons peppercorns
½ teaspoon cumin seeds
1½ cups water
1 (1-inch) piece fresh ginger
1½ tablespoons coarsely crushed rock sugar
4 holy basil leaves (optional)

1 Heat a cast-iron skillet or tava over medium heat. Add the peppercorns and dry roast for 30 to 40 seconds. Turn off the heat and add the cumin, stirring constantly for about a minute until a nice aroma emanates.

2 Remove and cool on a plate. Coarsely grind the mixture using a mortar and pestle or spice grinder.

3 In a saucepan, bring the water to a gentle boil and add the freshly ground spices, ginger, and sugar. Simmer for 10 minutes, or until the concoction reduces by half.

4 Remove from the heat, garnish with basil (if using), and serve.

Cooking Tip: The taste may be unfamiliar to those who have never had pepper in a drink, so you can reduce the amount of peppercorns by half if your spice threshold is low.

Substitution Tip: If you cannot get your hands on rock sugar, skip it completely. After the decoction is made and slightly cooled, add a teaspoon of honey and serve.

BUTTERMILK FOR DIGESTION

Chaas

ALL INDIA

VEGAN
GLUTEN-FREE
PEANUT-FREE
SOY-FREE
ALLIUM-FREE

SERVES 1 ◆ PREP TIME: 10 MINUTES *Indian buttermilk is a common digestive served after a meal. It not only cools the body, but the spices aid digestion and ward off acid reflux and gas. This simple buttermilk recipe is a great remedy for indigestion and is particularly soothing on a hot summer day, as it also prevents dehydration.*

½ cup thick plain yogurt
½ cup water
½ teaspoon Roasted Cumin Powder (page 42)
Kosher salt
½ teaspoon finely chopped cilantro leaves (optional)

1 Mix the yogurt vigorously with a little of the water so that no lumps remain. Add the cumin and season with salt.

2 Stir and gradually add the rest of the water to emulsify the water and yogurt completely.

3 Garnish with cilantro leaves (if using) and serve chilled.

Serving Tip: You can also add ice cubes for a more refreshing touch when serving. Always stir well before serving, since the water and yogurt tend to separate.

3

APPETIZERS AND SNACKS

CRISPY SPICED-POTATO SNACK

Aloo Chaat

NORTH INDIA

VEGAN
GLUTEN-FREE
PEANUT-FREE
SOY-FREE

SERVES 4 ♦ PREP TIME: 15 MINUTES ♦ COOK TIME: 20 MINUTES *Take a walk in Delhi, and the colors and aromas of street food shout out to you. Aloo chaat, deep-fried potatoes coated with an aromatic mixture of cilantro and cumin, is one of those street dishes that are difficult to ignore. With this simple recipe, you can bring the spicy, tangy, crunchy appeal of Indian street food to your kitchen in a matter of minutes.*

3 large potatoes (under 1 pound each)
Kosher salt
½ cup oil
4 tablespoons freshly squeezed lime juice
½ cup finely chopped red onion
2 tablespoons chopped cilantro leaves
½ teaspoon red chili powder
1 teaspoon Roasted Cumin Powder (page 42)
1 (½-inch) piece fresh ginger, slivered
1 teaspoon chaat masala (optional)
2 tablespoons Sweet and Sour Tamarind Chutney (page 109)
1 tablespoon Roasted Green Chile Chutney (page 116)

1 Wash the potatoes and cut them in half. Place in a large saucepan and cover with generously salted water. Bring to a boil over medium-high heat and cook until they are still firm but nearly cooked through, 10 to 15 minutes. Drain and cool. When the potatoes are cool enough to handle, peel and dice into cubes.

2 In a deep pot, heat the oil over medium-high heat. Lower the potatoes into the hot oil and fry until crisp and light brown. Remove using a slotted spoon, place the potatoes on a plate lined with paper towels to drain, and then transfer them to a large bowl.

3 In a small bowl, mix the lime juice, onion, cilantro, chili powder, and cumin powder. Toss with the potato pieces to coat.

4 Serve immediately, garnished with the ginger slivers and sprinkled with chaat masala (if using), with the chutneys on the side for dipping.

Cooking Tip: You can boil the potatoes in advance and fry them when you want to make this dish quickly. Or use leftover boiled potatoes from another dish to make the prep time even quicker.

Make It Healthier: Skip the deep frying and make this dish with boiled and cubed potatoes.

STUFFED-CHILE FRITTERS

Mirchi Vada

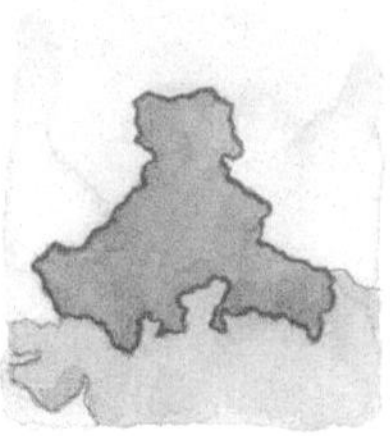

NORTH INDIA

VEGAN
GLUTEN-FREE
PEANUT-FREE
SOY-FREE
ALLIUM-FREE

SERVES 4 • PREP TIME: 15 MINUTES • COOK TIME: 10 MINUTES *I discovered these little flavor bombs while roaming the streets of Jaipur in Rajasthan. You'd think these fritters would be spicy, but they're actually quite mellow and have a lovely, comforting potato filling that's seasoned just right. You can use any broad chile, such as jalapeño or Anaheim, but don't substitute bell peppers—they have an entirely different flavor.*

FOR THE BATTER

½ cup chickpea flour
¼ teaspoon cumin seeds
¼ teaspoon kosher salt
½ teaspoon baking powder
¼ cup water

FOR THE STUFFED CHILES

1 cup boiled, peeled, mashed potatoes
¼ teaspoon red chili powder
¼ teaspoon ground cumin
1 teaspoon ground coriander
Kosher salt
8 whole chiles, slit lengthwise on one side and seeded, stems intact
Oil for deep frying

To make the batter

1 In a medium bowl, mix together the chickpea flour, cumin seeds, salt, and baking powder. Slowly add the water, while stirring constantly, to make a thick, smooth batter. You may need a little more or less water to achieve the right consistency.

2 Set the batter aside while you stuff the chiles.

To make the stuffed chiles

1 In a small bowl, mix together the potatoes, chili powder, cumin, coriander, and salt.

2 Spoon the stuffing into the slit chiles. Close the slit by gently pushing both ends together as much as possible without breaking the pepper. A little opening is fine.

3 In a deep pot, heat the oil over medium-high heat. Check if the oil is hot enough by dropping a bit of batter into it. If it sizzles, your oil is ready.

4 Dip the chiles into the batter until they are well coated. Shake off any excess and carefully transfer the chiles to the hot oil. Fry the chiles, turning them occasionally, until they are crisp and golden brown. Remove them to a plate lined with paper towels.

5 Serve immediately with Sweet and Sour Tamarind Chutney (page 109) or Cilantro and Mint Chutney (page 110).

Make It Healthier: Reduce the amount of oil used by shallow frying the peppers. If you go this route, just turn the peppers a little more frequently to ensure all sides are evenly fried.

Substitution Tip: I like to play around with the fillings of these peppers sometimes. A couple of my favorite additions to the potato filling are a little grated cheese or boiled, shelled prawns.

VEGETABLE PAKORAS

ALL INDIA

VEGAN
GLUTEN-FREE
PEANUT-FREE
SOY-FREE

SERVES 4 TO 5 • PREP TIME: 10 MINUTES • COOK TIME: 10 TO 12 MINUTES

Pakoras are perhaps one of the best-known Indian snacks around the world. Perfect for an impromptu get-together, the battered vegetables are typically served with a chutney to add some spice. Pakoras to me are synonymous with the Indian monsoon. There's nothing quite like having a plateful of these crisp veggies with a cup of tea while watching the rain beat down outside.

1 cup chickpea flour
1 teaspoon red chili powder
1 teaspoon carom seeds (optional)
1 teaspoon turmeric powder
Kosher salt
Water, for mixing
½ to 1 cup vegetable oil, for deep frying
1 medium potato, sliced very fine
1 small red onion, sliced very fine lengthwise
5 to 6 spinach leaves
1 green bell pepper cut into long, broad slices
½ cup blanched cauliflower florets

1 In a large bowl, mix together the chickpea flour, chili powder, carom seeds (if using), and turmeric. Season with salt. Add water, a little at a time until you have a pancake batter–like smooth consistency. Make sure there are no lumps. Adjust the salt.

2 In a deep saucepan, heat the oil until it shimmers. Check if the oil is hot enough by dropping in some batter. If it forms a ball and rises to the top, the oil is perfect for frying.

3 Dip the potato, onion, spinach, and bell pepper into the batter first. Fry them in batches until golden brown and crisp. Repeat with the cauliflower. Remove and transfer to a plated lined with paper towels. Serve hot with Masala Chai (page 227) and Sweet and Sour Tamarind Chutney (page 109) or Cilantro and Mint Chutney (page 110).

Substitution Tip: Use any vegetable or leafy green of your choice to make pakoras. Some possibilities include dill leaves, cabbage, corn, mushrooms, or even cubed slices of white bread.

SPICED FENUGREEK FLATBREAD

Methi Theplas

WEST AND CENTRAL INDIA

VEGETARIAN
EGG-FREE
PEANUT-FREE
SOY-FREE
ALLIUM-FREE

MAKES ABOUT 14 PIECES ◆ PREP TIME: 20 MINUTES ◆ COOK TIME: 15 MINUTES

I was introduced to these yummy flatbreads on a school picnic by one of my mates, whose mom had lovingly packed it for her. Fenugreek leaves are popular for their delicious taste and therapeutic value in Indian cuisine, and are said to control blood sugar, reduce cholesterol, and aid digestion. If you don't have fresh fenugreek, use cilantro instead. This will alter the taste, but it is another type of flatbread in its own right.

- 2 cups whole-wheat flour
- 1 teaspoon red chili powder
- 1 teaspoon Coriander-Cumin Spice Blend (page 43)
- ½ teaspoon turmeric powder
- 1 cup fenugreek leaves, removed from the stem and finely chopped
- 1 teaspoon carom seeds (optional)
- ¾ cup plain yogurt
- Kosher salt
- 4 tablespoons vegetable oil, divided

1 In a large bowl, mix together the flour, chili powder, coriander-cumin blend, turmeric, fenugreek leaves, and carom seeds (if using). Add the yogurt and a generous pinch of salt, and stir until the dough comes together.

2 Transfer the dough to a clean work surface and knead it until stiff. (The fenugreek may release some water into the dough; keep kneading until the dough is dry to the touch and does not stick to your work surface.) Add more yogurt or water if the dough is not coming together, but do so in small quantities. Add 2 tablespoons of oil to the dough and knead the dough briefly, just until the oil is incorporated.

3 Divide the dough into 14 equally sized pieces and roll each into a ball. Flour a work surface and, using a rolling pin, roll the balls into disks about 5 to 6 inches in diameter. continued ▶

SPICED FENUGREEK FLATBREAD *continued*

4 Heat a skillet or tava over high heat until it is nearly smoking and a drop of water sizzles and dances across the surface. In a small bowl, add the remaining 2 tablespoons of oil, and place it and a pastry brush near the skillet for easy access.

5 Place one disk of dough in the skillet. After a few seconds, gently lift it on one side with a fork or spatula. When brown bubbles appear on the bottom, brush some oil on top and flip the bread over. Brush the browned side with a little more oil. Flip the bread a couple of times until both sides have light golden brown spots on their surfaces. Remove the bread, and continue until all the flatbreads are cooked.

6 Serve the breads warm or at room temperature with plain yogurt or Mango Pickles (page 118). Or store them in an airtight container in the refrigerator for up to 3 days.

Make It Healthier: Reduce the whole-wheat flour to 1 cup and add ½ cup chickpea flour, ¼ cup sorghum flour, and ¼ cup pearl millet flour for a multigrain option.

Substitution Tip: To make this dairy-free and vegan, use 2 teaspoons lemon juice mixed with 1 tablespoon (or more as needed) water instead of the yogurt.

CHILE CHEESE TOAST

ALL INDIA

VEGETARIAN
EGG-FREE
PEANUT-FREE
SOY-FREE

SERVES 4 ◆ PREP TIME: 5 MINUTES ◆ COOK TIME: 10 MINUTES *This is a popular snack across India, served at breakfast and teatime. You'll also find it on the menus of restaurants and clubhouses, and it is very popular with kids. Use whole-wheat or multigrain bread instead of white for greater nutritional value. You can use more or less of the cheesy filling and add boiled vegetables, or—my favorite—ham!*

- 4 to 5 slices white bread
- Butter, at room temperature
- 1½ teaspoons vegetable oil
- 2 tablespoons finely chopped red onion (optional)
- 1 garlic clove, grated
- ½ cup grated Cheddar cheese (or any melting cheese)
- 1 green chile, finely chopped
- 1 tablespoon finely chopped bell pepper (optional)
- 1 tablespoon finely chopped cilantro leaves
- Kosher salt
- Olive oil

1 Butter the bread slices on both sides and lightly toast on a skillet or tava, or in the oven.

2 In a skillet, heat the oil over medium-high heat. Add the onion (if using) and garlic, stirring frequently for 1 minute to take away the rawness. Transfer to a bowl and add the cheese, chile, bell pepper (if using), cilantro, and salt. Drizzle a little olive oil into the mixture to make it spreadable.

3 Spread this mixture onto the toast. Arrange on a baking tray and broil the toast in the oven for 3 to 4 minutes, or until the cheese has melted.

4 Serve hot with tomato ketchup.

Substitution Tip: Some great additions to this cheese mixture are ham, bacon, or hardboiled eggs. Or choose a healthier option by topping the toast with boiled chopped vegetables, mushrooms, corn, or beans.

CHINESE CHILI PANEER

INDIAN-CHINESE

VEGETARIAN
EGG-FREE
GLUTEN-FREE
PEANUT-FREE

SERVES 2 ♦ PREP TIME: 15 MINUTES ♦ COOK TIME: 15 MINUTES *Indian-Chinese food probably started when Chinese and Indian flavors met during the spice trade, and was later adapted when Chinese settlers brought their culinary influences into eastern regions like Kolkatta. This dish plays on this unique fusion by combining Indian paneer with Chinese chili sauce to create a delicious result that goes well with both rice and noodles. If you have trouble purchasing paneer, there's a recipe for Homemade Paneer on page 140.*

FOR THE SAUCE

- 1 tablespoon cornstarch
- ¼ cup water
- 1 tablespoon dark soy sauce
- 1 tablespoon tomato ketchup
- 1½ teaspoons palm vinegar, coconut vinegar, or white vinegar (optional)
- 1 teaspoon Asian red chili sauce

FOR THE CHILI

- 1 tablespoon vegetable oil
- 1 tablespoon finely chopped garlic
- 1½ teaspoons finely chopped ginger
- 2 Thai red chiles, sliced lengthwise
- ½ cup chopped scallions, divided
- 1 cup thinly sliced red and/or green bell peppers
- Kosher salt
- 7 ounces paneer, cut in cubes

To make the sauce

In a small bowl, add the cornstarch and water. Mix well to form a paste. Add the soy sauce, ketchup, vinegar (if using), and red chili sauce, and mix well.

To make the chili

1 In a skillet, heat the oil over high heat and add the garlic, ginger, chiles, and all but 1 tablespoon of scallions. Cook, stirring constantly, until aromatic. Add the bell peppers and the sauce. Reduce the heat to medium and continue to cook until the sauce begins to thicken, 5 to 8 minutes. Check the seasoning and adjust the salt, but be careful because soy sauce is already salty.

2 Add the paneer cubes and stir to combine with the sauce. Sauté for a few minutes on high heat until the paneer is well combined and the sauce has formed a thick layer on the paneer.

3 Garnish with the reserved scallions and serve immediately.

Substitution Tip: Use tofu cubes instead of paneer for a vegan alternative. This sauce also works well with mushrooms, baby corn, blanched cauliflower florets, or boiled potato instead of paneer.

POTATO MASH WITH FRIED RED CHILES

Aloo Kangmet

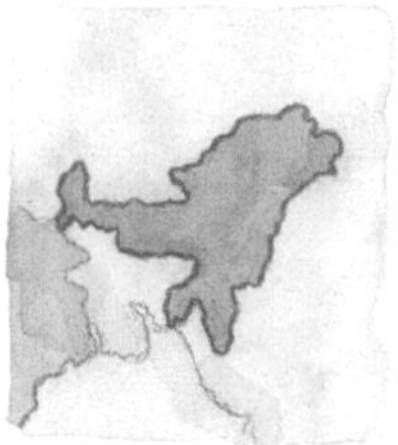

NORTHEAST INDIA

VEGAN
GLUTEN-FREE
PEANUT-FREE
SOY-FREE

SERVES 2 • PREP TIME: 10 MINUTES • COOK TIME: 10 MINUTES *If you've ever wondered how to give the humble mashed potato a twist, look no further. This simple recipe cooks up a potent mash that will leave you wanting more. I like how the crunch from the fried onions adds a nice texture to the mash, and how the little bits of chile play hide and seek with your taste buds with every morsel.*

- 1 tablespoon vegetable oil
- 6 dried red chiles
- 1 small red onion, thinly sliced
- 1 cup boiled, peeled, and mashed potatoes
- Kosher salt
- 1 tablespoon chopped cilantro leaves (optional)

1 In a frying pan or saucepan, heat the oil on medium heat until it's shimmering. Reduce the heat to low and fry the dried chiles until they turn a deeper brown. Keep turning them frequently to prevent blackening, as they take very little time to go from red to brown. Remove, drain, and cool. When cool, break the chiles into smaller bits.

2 In the same oil, fry the onion slices until almost crisp. Remove, drain, and cool.

3 In a large bowl, mix the mashed potatoes, fried red chile bits, and onion. Season with salt and garnish with cilantro (if using). Serve as a side to any Indian vegetarian meal, with Amritsari Flatbread (page 94), or as an amped-up side dish to a Western-style meal.

Cooking Tip: When you are frying chiles, stand back from the stove to avoid breathing the vapors produced, which can cause sneezing and coughing.

ANDHRA EGG PEPPER FRY

Muttai Milagu

SOUTH INDIA

VEGETARIAN
DAIRY-FREE
GLUTEN-FREE
PEANUT-FREE
SOY-FREE

SERVES 4 • PREP TIME: 10 MINUTES • COOK TIME: 15 MINUTES *Andhra food is famous for its spicy kick, and this dish is no exception. As you bite into it, you will find the egg itself mellows the sharpness of the spice, giving it a lovely balance, while the rice flour gives the eggs a subtle crunchiness.*

- 2 to 3 tablespoons rice flour
- 2 teaspoons Ginger-Garlic Paste (page 46)
- 1 teaspoon red chili powder or flakes
- 2 teaspoons freshly ground black pepper
- ¼ teaspoon turmeric powder
- 1 sprig (about 10 to 12) curry leaves, torn into small pieces (optional)
- Kosher salt
- Water, for mixing
- 4 eggs, hardboiled, peeled, halved lengthwise
- 2 to 3 tablespoons vegetable oil

1. In a bowl, mix together the rice flour, ginger-garlic paste, chili powder, pepper, turmeric, curry leaves (if using), and salt. Add a few drops of water to form a thick paste. Rub this mixture over the hardboiled eggs, adding a little extra to the cut sides.

2. In a skillet, heat the oil over medium-low heat. Place the eggs in the hot oil with the cut side down. Fry until evenly golden brown and flip to brown the rounded side.

3. Remove and place on a plate lined with paper towels to remove excess oil. Serve the eggs hot with any sliced bread or on their own.

Ingredient Tip: Dried or frozen curry leaves work well in this recipe. Just tear them in small pieces and increase the quantity by half.

Cooking Tip: You can reduce the amount of heat in the dish by omitting the red chili powder or halving the black pepper, but do not omit the pepper altogether.

BENGALI FISH CROQUETTES

Macher Chop

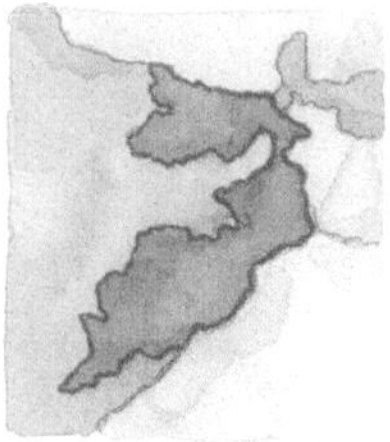

EAST INDIA

DAIRY-FREE
PEANUT-FREE
SOY-FREE

MAKES 10 TO 12 PIECES ◆ PREP TIME: 20 MINUTES, PLUS 20 MINUTES TO MARINATE ◆ COOK TIME: 35 MINUTES *In Indian cuisine, a nonvegetarian croquette usually refers to a minced meat patty, either round or flat, dredged in egg and breadcrumbs and fried. These macher chops from West Bengal are crisp on the outside and soft and hearty inside. Dip them into sharp bengali kasundi (mustard sauce), and you're guaranteed to be transported to foodie heaven.*

FOR THE MARINADE

Juice of 1 lime
1 tablespoon Ginger-Garlic Paste (page 46)
Kosher salt
½ teaspoon red chili powder (optional)
1 pound barramundi fish fillets (or any firm, white-fleshed fish fillets)

FOR THE FISH

1 tablespoon vegetable oil
3 tablespoons finely chopped garlic
½ cup finely chopped red onion
3 green chiles, finely chopped

FOR THE PATTIES

¾ cup mashed potatoes
2 tablespoons finely chopped cilantro leaves and stems
1 teaspoon ground cumin
1 teaspoon freshly ground black pepper
2 tablespoons vegetable oil
½ cup to 1 cup all-purpose flour
1 egg, beaten
1 cup breadcrumbs

To make the marinade

1 In a large bowl, mix together the lime juice, ginger-garlic paste, salt, and chili powder (if using).

2 Add the fish and toss to coat. Season with salt. Cover and refrigerate for 20 minutes.

To cook the fish

1 In a small skillet, heat 1 tablespoon oil over medium heat. Add the garlic and cook, stirring continuously, until it becomes fragrant. Add the onion and continue stirring until softened, 8 to 10 minutes. Add the chiles and continue cooking until fragrant.

2 Add the fish to the pan, discarding any marinade remaining in the bowl. Stir continuously and use the spoon to break the fish apart into small pieces. Continue to cook for 2 to 3 minutes. Turn off the heat and transfer the fish mixture to a bowl to cool.

To make the patties

1 Drain any excess liquid that accumulated in the bowl while cooling, and discard. Stir in the potatoes, cilantro, ground cumin, and pepper. Stir well until the mixture is smooth. Adjust seasonings as needed.

2 Using your hands, shape the mixture into 10 to 12 patties measuring about 2 inches in diameter and ½ inch thick.

3 Heat 2 tablespoons of oil in a large skillet over medium heat.

4 Place the flour, egg, and breadcrumbs on separate plates. Dredge each patty in flour, shaking off any excess, then dredge it in the egg, and, finally, roll it in the breadcrumbs.

5 Add half of the patties to the hot skillet and fry until golden brown. Flip and fry the other side until it is brown and crisp as well, 3 to 5 minutes per side. Remove the cooked patties to a plate lined with paper towels. Repeat until all the patties are cooked. Serve immediately with mustard sauce or ketchup.

Make It Faster: If you don't have leftover mashed potatoes for this recipe, you can prepare them in the pressure cooker. Peel and quarter one medium russet potato and steam according to your pressure cooker instructions for 9 minutes. Let the pressure release naturally, then remove the potato with tongs and mash or rice until smooth.

Ingredient Tip: Avoid using oily fish like tuna or pink-fleshed fish like salmon. You want to use a white-fleshed fish that doesn't have an overpowering taste.

SHRIMP KEBABS

Kolmi na Kavaab

WEST AND CENTRAL INDIA

DAIRY-FREE
PEANUT-FREE

SERVES 4 ◆ PREP TIME: 20 MINUTES, PLUS 10 MINUTES TO REST ◆ COOK TIME: 10 MINUTES *With ancestry in ancient Iran, the Zoroastrian Parsis made Gujarat and later Mumbai in Maharashtra their home. Their cuisine has evolved into a unique mix of Iranian influences and Indian spices and techniques, and is popular throughout the country. This delicious appetizer is mildly spiced, so the flavor of the shrimp truly shines.*

1 pound medium shrimp, shelled and deveined
½ teaspoon turmeric powder
2 teaspoons freshly ground black pepper
2 teaspoons Coriander-Cumin Spice Blend (page 43)
½ teaspoon red chili powder
1 tablespoon chopped cilantro leaves
1 small green chile, finely chopped
1 medium potato, peeled, boiled, and mashed
1 slice bread, dipped in water and squeezed dry
Kosher salt
1 tablespoon Worcestershire sauce
1 teaspoon palm vinegar, coconut vinegar, or white vinegar
1 egg, beaten
2 tablespoons vegetable oil

1 Place the shrimp in a food processor and pulse until finely chopped, about 10 short pulses, or chop finely by hand. Transfer to a large bowl.

2 Add the turmeric, pepper, coriander-cumin blend, chili powder, cilantro, chile, potato, bread, salt, Worcestershire sauce, vinegar, and egg. Mix well. Refrigerate and allow the mixture to rest for about 10 minutes.

3 In a heavy-bottomed nonstick skillet, heat the oil over high heat until it's shimmering. Lower the heat to medium-low.

4 Wet your hands with some water so the mix doesn't stick. Using a tablespoon, scoop out the shrimp mixture into your palm and shape the spoonfuls into rounds. Lower the rounds gently into the hot oil, standing a little away from the pan. Fry until golden brown on both sides, about 5 minutes total, flipping once or twice to create even browning. Transfer to a paper towel–lined plate to drain. Repeat until all the patties are cooked.

Serving Tip: Serve with Cilantro and Mint Chutney (page 110) or tomato sauce as a starter, or with a main meal as a side dish.

CRUMB-FRIED MUTTON CHOPS

ANGLO-INDIAN

DAIRY-FREE
PEANUT-FREE
SOY-FREE

SERVES 4 ◆ PREP TIME: 20 MINUTES, PLUS 30 MINUTES TO OVERNIGHT TO MARINATE ◆ COOK TIME: 35 MINUTES *This is a classic Anglo-Indian preparation that marries the spices of India with the cooking technique of crumb frying that was prevalent during the Raj, or colonial rule. Mutton or goat meat is widely used in India and is more robust in flavor than lamb.*

FOR THE CHOPS
2 pounds bone-in goat or lamb chops
1 tablespoon freshly ground black pepper
1 teaspoon turmeric powder
Kosher salt

FOR THE SPICE MIXTURE
4 tablespoons vegetable oil, divided
1 medium red onion, finely sliced
4 garlic cloves, finely chopped
1 (1-inch) piece fresh ginger, finely chopped
3 green Serrano chiles, cut in half lengthwise
4 peppercorns
2 whole cloves
1 Indian bay leaf or Mediterranean bay leaf
2 cups water
1 egg, beaten
1 cup fresh breadcrumbs

To make the chops

1 In a large bowl, toss the chops with the pepper and turmeric. Season with salt.

2 Set aside for at least 30 minutes, or overnight if you have the time.

To make the spice mixture

1 In a heavy-bottomed saucepan, heat 1 tablespoon of oil over medium heat until it begins to shimmer. Add the onion, garlic, ginger, and chiles and cook, stirring often, until fragrant and softened but not browned.

2 Add the peppercorns, cloves, and bay leaf, and stir until fragrant, about 2 minutes longer.

3 Add the chops and cook them in the spice mixture until they are lightly browned, 3 to 5 minutes per side. Pour in the water and bring it to a boil, then reduce the heat to low, cover, and simmer until the chops are cooked through, 20 to 25 minutes. The chops are done when an instant-read thermometer inserted into the meatiest part registers 145°F.

4 Remove the chops from the pan and set them aside on a plate. Retain the stock in the saucepan to use in curries, pilafs, or as a hearty soup. (The leftover stock will keep in an airtight container in the refrigerator for up to 5 days, or in the freezer for up to 5 months.)

5 Place the egg on a plate and spread the breadcrumbs on another plate. Heat the remaining 3 tablespoons of oil in a frying pan or skillet over high heat until it begins to shimmer. Dip each chop into the egg and then coat it evenly with the breadcrumbs. Reduce the heat to medium-high and place the chops in the oil. Fry the chops for 5 to 7 minutes total, turning them occasionally to ensure that all sides are evenly golden brown and crunchy. Serve hot.

Make It Faster: Cook the chops and spice mixture in an electric pressure cooker for 15 minutes on high pressure. Release the pressure naturally.

STUFFED POTATO CAKES

Potato Chops

WEST AND CENTRAL INDIA

DAIRY-FREE
GLUTEN-FREE
PEANUT-FREE
SOY-FREE

SERVES 4 ◆ PREP TIME: 20 MINUTES ◆ COOK TIME: 30 MINUTES *These delicate stuffed potato cakes from Goa make a delicious appetizer or side. Minced lamb or beef is spiced and stuffed into a mashed potato cake, breaded, and fried. The result is a lovely mix of textures—crunchy and soft. I like to serve it with ketchup or any Indian chutney, and make extra for leftovers the next day.*

FOR THE STUFFING

1 cup ground beef or lamb
2 teaspoons Ginger-Garlic Paste (page 46)
1½ tablespoons vegetable oil
½ cup finely chopped red onion
2 tablespoons tomato purée
1 tablespoon Roasted Cumin Powder (page 42)
1 teaspoon turmeric powder
½ tablespoon red chili powder
½ teaspoon freshly ground black pepper
½ tablespoon malt vinegar
1 teaspoon sugar
Kosher salt
1 tablespoon chopped cilantro leaves
¼ cup water

FOR THE POTATO CAKES

2 cups cooked mashed potatoes
2 eggs, beaten
1 cup fine breadcrumbs
4 tablespoons vegetable oil

To make the stuffing

1 In a large bowl, mix the ground meat and ginger-garlic paste. Set aside.

2 In a medium saucepan, heat the oil over medium heat until it is shimmering. Add the chopped onion and cook, stirring occasionally, until it is lightly softened, about 2 minutes. Add the tomato purée and cook, stirring frequently, until it is reduced and the oil comes up to the surface, about 3 minutes.

3 Add the cumin powder, turmeric, chili powder, and pepper. Cook, stirring constantly, until fragrant, about 1 minute. Add the vinegar and stir to incorporate.

4 Add the sugar, salt, and meat. Cook until the meat is coated in the spice mixture and cooked through, and oil rises to the surface, about 8 minutes. Add the cilantro and water. Cover and cook for 10 minutes. Remove the cover and continue cooking until all the water is completely evaporated. Season with salt, then cool.

To make the potato cakes

1 Shape the potatoes into rounds about 2½ inches in diameter and ½ inch thick.

2 Put one round in the palm of your hand and make a shallow indentation in the center. Add 1 tablespoon of the meat filling. Gently fold the sides of the potato round over the filling until it is completely covered. Gently flatten into a disk. Repeat with the remaining potatoes and filling.

3 Dip each potato cake into the egg and dredge in breadcrumbs, then transfer to a clean large plate. Heat the oil in a medium nonstick skillet over medium heat until it is shimmering. Gently slide the potato cakes into the oil and fry on both sides until lightly golden brown, about 1 minute on each side. Drain on absorbent kitchen towels and serve with any chutney or sauce of your choice.

Substitution Tip: You can make this vegetarian by using crumbled paneer or chopped mushrooms instead of meat in the stuffing. Cook them exactly the same way as the meat.

4

RICE, GRAINS, AND BREADS

PLAIN BASMATI RICE

ALL INDIA

VEGAN
GLUTEN-FREE
PEANUT-FREE
SOY-FREE
ALLIUM-FREE

SERVES 2 • PREP TIME: 5 MINUTES • COOK TIME: 15 TO 18 MINUTES *This is the basic white rice that is made across India. I use ½ cup of raw rice per person and twice as much water as rice, so you can modify the recipe using these basic measures. Remember to wash the rice to remove any residue, reduce starchiness, and help the grains cook separately.*

1 cup raw basmati rice
2 cups water
Kosher salt

1 Put the rice in a bowl and fill the bowl with water. Run your fingers through the rice, then pour the water off through a fine-mesh strainer. Do this two or three times; the water will get less and less cloudy with each wash.

2 Bring the 2 cups of water to a boil in a saucepan over medium heat. Add a generous amount of salt.

3 Add the washed and drained rice, and stir. Reduce the heat to medium-low. Cover the saucepan with a lid. Cook for 15 to 18 minutes.

4 When you open the lid, you will notice steam pockets that have formed in the rice. The water should have totally dried up. If not, cover and cook for a few more minutes. Use a fork to gently stir the cooked rice, so as not to break the grains.

Ingredient Tip: Some basmati brands say "aged" on the label. If so, reduce the amount of water by about 2 tablespoons from the standard ratio of 1 cup rice to 2 cups water.

AROMATIC YELLOW RICE

ALL INDIA

VEGAN
GLUTEN-FREE
PEANUT-FREE
SOY-FREE

SERVES 2 ◆ PREP TIME: 10 MINUTES ◆ COOK TIME: 18 TO 20 MINUTES *I love the bright yellow color of this rice dish—a reminder of the vibrancy of Indian food. I prefer to use a long-grain or basmati rice, but you can use any rice variety except sticky rice or short-grain glutinous rice, because you will end up with a starchy, sticky mess.*

1 tablespoon vegetable oil
1 small red onion, sliced
2 whole cloves
1 (1-inch) cinnamon stick
2 cardamom pods, bruised
1 Indian bay leaf or Mediterranean bay leaf
1 teaspoon turmeric powder
1 teaspoon sugar
2 tablespoons fresh or frozen peas (optional)
1 cup basmati rice, washed
2 cups water
Kosher salt

1 In a medium saucepan, heat the oil over medium heat until it is shimmering. Add the onion and sauté until it begins to brown, about 5 minutes. Add the cloves, cinnamon, cardamom, and bay leaf, and stir till aromatic, about 5 minutes. Add the turmeric and sugar, and stir briskly to ensure the turmeric doesn't burn. Add the peas (if using) and rice, and stir to coat with the flavored oil for about a minute.

2 Add the water and salt and stir. Reduce the heat to medium-low. Cover the saucepan with a lid. Allow to cook for 15 to 18 minutes.

3 When you open the lid, you will notice steam pockets that have formed in the rice. The water should have totally dried up. If not, cover and cook for a few more minutes. Use a fork to gently stir the cooked rice so as not to break the grains. Serve with any main dish.

Ingredient Tip: If you're using fresh peas, increase the water by about 2 tablespoons to make sure the peas cook through.

LIME RICE

Elumichai Sadam

SOUTH INDIA

VEGAN
GLUTEN-FREE
SOY-FREE
ALLIUM-FREE

SERVES 2 ◆ PREP TIME: 15 MINUTES ◆ COOK TIME: 10 MINUTES *In most Indian homes there's always some leftover cooked rice in the refrigerator, and that's just what you need for this recipe. (You can use freshly made rice as well; just be sure to cool the rice completely, or you may end up with a sticky mess.) The mixture of lentils, curry leaves, chiles, peanuts, and turmeric is balanced with lime juice to give this dish a tangy, savory taste.*

- 1½ tablespoons vegetable oil
- 2 to 3 green chiles, split in half lengthwise
- 1 teaspoon black mustard seeds
- 1 teaspoon husked black lentils (urad dal)
- 1 teaspoon split yellow chickpeas (Bengal gram)
- 2 tablespoons roasted peanuts
- 8 to 10 fresh curry leaves or 15 dried or frozen curry leaves (optional)
- 1 teaspoon turmeric powder
- 2½ tablespoons freshly squeezed lime juice
- Kosher salt
- 1½ cups cooked and chilled white rice
- 1 teaspoon sugar
- 10 cashews, fried in a little oil until light brown, for garnish (optional)

1 In a cast-iron skillet or kadhai, heat the oil over medium heat until it's shimmering. Add the chiles, stand back, and stir for a few seconds until fragrant. Add the mustard seeds and stir for a few seconds until they pop. Quickly add the lentils, chickpeas, and peanuts. Continue stirring until the dal turns a light brown, about 5 minutes.

2 Add the curry leaves (if using). Stir until fragrant, about 30 seconds. Add the turmeric and stir for a few seconds, taking care not to burn it. Turn the heat off and add the lime juice and a pinch of salt, stirring to combine.

3 Add the rice and sugar to the warm oil. Fold the rice gently to keep the rice intact, or use a fork for stirring, as it doesn't break the rice grains while folding. Stir until well combined and all the ingredients are incorporated.

4 Serve warm, garnished with the fried cashews if desired.

Substitution Tip: If you have a peanut allergy, either omit the peanuts altogether or use flaked almonds or cashews instead.

RICE AND LENTIL ONE-POT MEAL

Oriya Khichudi

EAST INDIA

FESTIVAL FOOD

VEGAN
GLUTEN-FREE
PEANUT-FREE
SOY-FREE
ALLIUM-FREE

SERVES 4 ♦ PREP TIME: 15 MINUTES ♦ COOK TIME: 30 MINUTES *During the Hindu festival of Durga Puja, Bengali and Oriya families make this special rice and lentil dish as an offering to the goddess. After the offering, it is served to the rest of the congregation as a nourishing meal for body and soul. Khichudi is a very nutritious, mellow, and comforting one-pot meal, which is delicious with any combination of vegetables.*

3 tablespoons ghee or 2 tablespoons vegetable oil, divided
1 tablespoon cumin seeds
2 to 3 dried red chiles, broken in half
3 Indian bay leaves or Mediterranean bay leaves
1 (1-inch) piece fresh ginger, slivered
½ teaspoon asafetida
1 teaspoon turmeric powder
1 cup rice
1 cup split yellow mung beans (moong dal)
½ cup finely chopped carrot
½ cup chopped potato
½ cup peas
1 medium tomato, chopped
Kosher salt
4 cups water
2 teaspoons sugar
⅓ cup raisins

1 In a heavy saucepan with a lid, heat 2 tablespoons of ghee until it's shimmering. Add the cumin seeds, chiles, bay leaves, and ginger, and sauté until the seeds crackle. Add the asafetida and turmeric and stir for no longer than 10 seconds.

2 Add the rice, mung beans, carrot, potato, peas, and tomato. Stir together with the flavored ghee. Season with salt. Add the water, sugar, and raisins. Stir again.

3 When the mixture starts to simmer, cover and cook over medium heat for about 25 minutes. Check once while cooking to see if the water has dried out. If so, add more to ensure that the beans and rice are cooked completely. The consistency of the khichudi should be rather mushy, like a risotto, so if the grains are slightly broken or the khichudi is a bit runny, it's okay. Serve hot with a garnish of the remaining ghee (do not garnish with vegetable oil) and a side of Spiced Fried Eggplant (page 159).

Make It Faster: Mix 2 tablespoons of ghee with the cumin seeds, red chiles, bay leaves, and ginger in an electric pressure cooker and heat on the Sauté setting for 30 seconds. Stir in the asafetida, then the turmeric, rice, beans, sugar, raisins, and vegetables; pour in 2½ cups of water. Stir, bring to a simmer, and close the lid; pressure cook for 10 minutes at high pressure. Use the quick method to release the pressure.

Cooking Tip: If you plan to leave out all the vegetables in this dish except the tomatoes, reduce the quantity of water by ½ cup.

SZECHUAN FRIED BASMATI RICE

INDIAN-CHINESE

VEGAN
GLUTEN-FREE
PEANUT-FREE

SERVES 4 ◆ PREP TIME: 15 MINUTES ◆ COOK TIME: 10 MINUTES *I keep a jar of Szechuan Chutney (page 117) in my refrigerator at all times so I can whip up a batch of this tasty dish whenever I have leftover rice. To make things easy, prep all your vegetables ahead of time and place them in bowls within arm's reach of the stove.*

2 tablespoons vegetable oil
1 (1-inch) piece fresh ginger, grated
3 garlic cloves, finely chopped
3 scallions, white and green parts chopped and kept separate
2 cups combined chopped or shredded carrots, green beans, cabbage, and green, red, or yellow bell peppers
2 teaspoons light soy sauce
½ teaspoon palm vinegar, coconut vinegar, or white vinegar
2 tablespoons Szechuan Chutney (page 117)
1½ cups cooked and chilled basmati rice
Kosher salt

1 In a cast-iron skillet, wok, or kadhai, heat the oil over medium heat until it's shimmering. Add the ginger, garlic, and the white parts of the scallions and fry until the rawness in the aroma disappears, taking care not to brown anything.

2 Add the vegetables and half the scallion greens. Stir and cook until the vegetables are tender. Add the soy sauce, vinegar, and Szechuan chutney, and mix well.

3 Add the cooled rice and stir carefully to combine the sauces, rice, and vegetables. Check the seasonings and adjust. Season with salt. Serve hot, garnished with the reserved scallion greens and a side like Chinese Chili Paneer (page 62).

Cooking Tip: Add cubed chicken, bacon, ham, whole shrimp, or even lightly beaten eggs before the vegetables. Cook thoroughly and then continue with step 2, adding the vegetables and sauces.

HYDERABADI LAMB BIRYANI

SOUTH INDIA

GLUTEN-FREE
PEANUT-FREE
SOY-FREE

SERVES 6 TO 7 ♦ PREP TIME: 30 MINUTES, PLUS 3 HOURS TO OVERNIGHT TO MARINATE ♦ COOK TIME: 2 HOURS *There are many types of biryanis in India, and they vary according to region in both flavors and method. This recipe is from Hyderabad, where there are two ways to make biryani: by cooking the meat and the rice together in a sealed pot, or this way, by starting the meat and rice separately and then arranging them in layers to finish cooking together.*

FOR THE MARINADE

4 tablespoons vegetable oil
2 cups sliced red onions
2 tablespoons chopped cilantro leaves
2 tablespoons mint leaves
2 green chiles, chopped
2 tablespoons Ginger-Garlic Paste (page 46)
1 cup plain thick yogurt
Kosher salt
1 tablespoon red chili powder
1 tablespoon turmeric powder
3½ pounds bone-in lamb chops

FOR THE LAMB

2 tablespoons ghee *or* vegetable oil
1 medium red onion, chopped
2 Indian bay leaves or Mediterranean bay leaves
2 teaspoons Basic Homemade Garam Masala (page 44)
4 tablespoons freshly squeezed lime juice
2 tablespoons finely chopped cilantro leaves
2 tablespoons finely chopped mint leaves

FOR THE RICE

4 cups basmati rice
8 cups water
3 whole cloves
4 green cardamom pods
2 cinnamon sticks
1 tablespoon caraway seeds
4 peppercorns
Kosher salt
1 pinch saffron strands mixed in 2 tablespoons warm water or milk

FOR THE BIRYANI

1 tablespoon ghee or vegetable oil, plus more as needed
3 tablespoons finely chopped cilantro leaves
3 tablespoons finely chopped mint leaves
2 green chiles, chopped
2 hardboiled eggs cut in quarters (optional)
2 tablespoon toasted slivered almonds (optional)

continued ▸

To make the marinade

1 In a saucepan, heat the oil on medium heat until it is shimmering, and fry the onion slices until golden brown. They should be fried crisp. Drain on absorbent paper and cool.

2 Using a spice grinder or mortar and pestle, grind the cilantro, mint, and chiles to a paste.

3 Scoop the paste into a small bowl and stir in 1 tablespoon of the fried onions (reserve the rest), the ginger-garlic paste, yogurt, salt, chili powder, and turmeric. Rub this mixture all over the lamb, then transfer the lamb to an airtight container and marinate in the refrigerator for at least 3 hours or overnight.

To make the lamb

1 In a large, heavy saucepan, heat the ghee over medium heat until it is shimmering. Add the chopped onion and fry until it is golden brown. Add the bay leaves and marinated meat, and cook until the oil separates, about 10 minutes.

2 Add the garam masala and enough water to just cover the meat. Cover the pot and cook for about 45 minutes, until the gravy has become thick, the oil has separated, and the meat is tender. (Cooking time depends on the size of the lamb pieces and how long you've marinated it.)

3 In the last 5 minutes of cooking, add the lime juice, cilantro, and mint, and mix well.

To make the rice

1 While the lamb cooks, wash the rice and soak it in water for about 30 minutes; drain and rinse the rice.

2 Pour 8 cups of cold water into a large pot, along with the cloves, cardamom, cinnamon, caraway seeds, peppercorns, and salt. Let it come to a boil and add the drained rice. Give it a stir and let the rice cook until it is half done, 10 to 12 minutes. Drain the rice and set it aside.

3 Put about one-quarter of the rice in a medium bowl and pour over the saffron mixture to color it yellow. Keep this separate.

To make the biryani

1 Spread the ghee over the bottom of a large pot and spread out a layer of about 2 inches of the half-cooked rice. Then add a layer of the lamb to cover the rice. Add some of the reserved fried onions from the marinade, along with some of the cilantro, mint, and chiles, and a spot of ghee or a drizzle of oil. Add another layer of rice, then the rest of the lamb, reserved fried onions, and herbs. Finish with the saffron rice on top.

2 Cover the pot with aluminum foil and then a lid, and place over low heat for 15 to 30 minutes to cook the biryani in its own steam. Switch off the heat but do not open the pot. Allow the biryani to rest for at least 15 minutes before opening and serving. Garnish with hardboiled eggs and slivered almonds, if you like, and serve with Cooling Yogurt and Vegetable Salad (page 104).

Substitution Tip: You can use cut-up, bone-in, skinless chicken instead of lamb. The chicken should be cooked for about 30 minutes on low heat.

QUICK MEAT PILAF

Junglee Pulav

ANGLO-INDIAN

EGG-FREE
GLUTEN-FREE
PEANUT-FREE

SERVES 4 TO 5 ♦ PREP TIME: 10 MINUTES ♦ COOK TIME: 30 MINUTES

Junglee *literally translates as "wild" in English. This is classic Anglo-Indian humor to personify a dish that is actually a wild mishmash of ingredients that are commonly found in the Indian pantry. It is often made with leftover meat or vegetable curry, which gives a new lease on life to yesterday's dinner.*

- 2 tablespoons vegetable oil or ghee
- 1 large red onion, sliced thin
- 1 (2-inch) cinnamon stick
- 4 whole cloves
- 3 green cardamom pods
- 2 Indian bay leaves or Mediterranean bay leaves
- 2 teaspoons ground coriander
- ½ teaspoon turmeric powder
- 3 teaspoons red chili powder or paprika
- 1 tablespoon Ginger-Garlic Paste (page 46)
- 1½ teaspoons Basic Homemade Garam Masala (page 44)
- 2 cups basmati or any long-grain rice
- Kosher salt
- ½ cup fresh peas (optional)
- 1 small potato, diced (optional)
- 1 carrot, diced fine (optional)
- 1 cup leftover vegetable, chickpea, kidney bean, or meat-based curry (anything except lentils)
- 1½ cups water or beef, chicken, or vegetable stock

1 Heat the oil in a heavy saucepan over medium heat. Add the onion and sauté until softened. Add the cinnamon, cloves, cardamom, and bay leaves. Sauté until the onion is golden brown and the spices are aromatic, about 8 minutes.

2 Reduce the heat to low. Add the coriander, turmeric, and chili powder, stir vigorously for 30 seconds, then stir in the ginger-garlic paste and garam masala; cook for 5 minutes longer.

3 Stir in the rice and season with salt.

4 Add the peas, potato, and carrot (if using), and the leftover curry and water, and increase the heat to medium. When the stock simmers, return the heat to low, cover the pan, and cook until all the moisture is absorbed, 12 to 15 minutes. If the liquid is drying up too quickly, add ¼ cup water or stock and stir with the handle of the spoon so as not to break the rice grains. Turn off the heat once the rice is tender.

5 Uncover the pan and allow the rice to air dry for about 5 minutes before fluffing. Serve hot with Cooling Yogurt and Vegetable Salad (page 104).

Make It Faster: Follow steps 1 through 4, using the pressure cooker as the cooking pot. After you add the rice, seal the lid and pressure cook for 7 minutes at high pressure. Release the pressure naturally. The ratio of rice to liquid should be 1 cup dry rice to 1½ cups liquid. If you're using vegetables like potato and carrot, increase the liquid by ¼ cup.

Substitution Tip: You can add any vegetable of your choice if you don't like carrots, peas, or potatoes. Just remember to cut them the same size as the other vegetables to ensure even cooking time.

MILLET PILAF

Veg Pulav

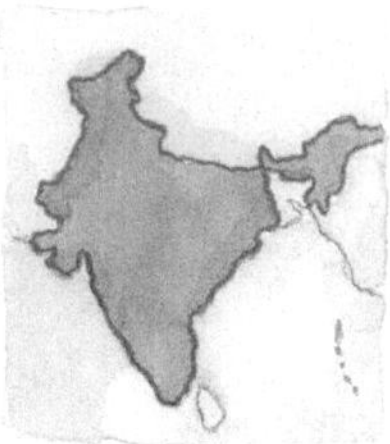

ALL INDIA

VEGAN
GLUTEN-FREE
PEANUT-FREE
SOY-FREE

SERVES 2 ◆ PREP TIME: 20 MINUTES ◆ COOK TIME: 25 MINUTES *Pilafs (or pulavs, as they are called in India) have a staggering number of variations. They can be vegan or meat-based, and made with rice or any other grain. Once you master it, you'll find that this basic pilaf recipe works well with just about anything.*

1 cup millet
1 tablespoon vegetable oil
1 teaspoon cumin seeds
1 teaspoon fennel seeds
1 (½-inch) cinnamon stick
2 lightly bruised green cardamom pods
2 whole cloves
1 star anise
1 Indian bay leaf or Mediterranean bay leaf
5 to 6 peppercorns
1 small red onion, finely sliced
2 teaspoons Ginger-Garlic Paste (page 46)
1 small potato, peeled and chopped
1 small carrot, peeled and chopped
¼ cup fresh or frozen peas
2 green chiles, split in half lengthwise
¼ cup cauliflower, broken into small florets
1 teaspoon Roasted Cumin Powder (page 42) (optional)
2 cups water or coconut milk
1 tablespoon chopped cilantro leaves
Kosher salt

1 Rinse the millet and soak it in a bowl of cold water for at least 10 minutes.

2 In a saucepan or kadhai, heat the oil over medium heat until it's shimmering. Add the cumin and fennel, stirring until they crackle. In quick succession, add the cinnamon, cardamom, cloves, star anise, bay leaf, and peppercorns. Stir until fragrant, about 30 seconds.

3 Add the onion and sauté on medium-low until golden brown and softened. Add the ginger-garlic paste and stir until fragrant.

4 Add the potato, carrot, peas, chiles, and cauliflower and sauté for 1 minute. Stir in the millet and cumin powder (if using), then add the water and cilantro. Season with salt.

5 Cover and cook on low for 15 to 20 minutes, until the millet is tender. The pilaf is ready when the water has dried up and the vegetables and millet are cooked through. If the liquid is drying up too fast, use a fork to stir the grains and add more water, ¼ cup at a time. Serve hot with Cooling Yogurt and Vegetable Salad (page 104) and any other Indian side.

Substitution Tip: To make this a rice pilaf, use 1 cup unsoaked rice instead of millet, and add ¼ cup more water or coconut milk. Cooking time will increase by 5 minutes.

Substitution Tip: If you like, you can add cooked meat to this dish, such as ground lamb or chicken pieces.

AROMATIC SHRIMP PILAF

Kolambi Bhaat

WEST AND CENTRAL INDIA

EGG-FREE
DAIRY-FREE
GLUTEN-FREE
PEANUT-FREE
SOY-FREE

SERVES 2 ◆ PREP TIME: 20 MINUTES ◆ COOK TIME: 30 MINUTES *Rice is a weakness for me, and if it's coupled with a seafood, I'm not moving far from the plate. Kolambi bhaat is an aromatic pilaf from Maharashtra that uses fragrant spices and fresh shrimp. This is a wonderful, quick dish to prepare for the family or for a dinner party, and one that is different from the usual Indian biryanis and pilafs.*

- 1½ cups medium shrimp, peeled and deveined
- 2 teaspoons turmeric powder
- 1 tablespoon freshly squeezed lime juice
- 1 teaspoon Ginger-Garlic Paste (page 46)
- 2 tablespoons fresh, or frozen and thawed, grated coconut
- 2 tablespoons tomato purée or 2 medium tomatoes, chopped
- 3 to 4 green chiles, halved lengthwise, stemmed
- 2 teaspoons red chili powder
- 2 tablespoons chopped cilantro leaves and tender stems
- 1 garlic clove, finely chopped
- 1 (½-inch) piece fresh ginger, grated
- 2 tablespoons water
- 3 tablespoons canola oil
- 4 whole cloves
- 1 (2-inch) cinnamon stick
- 3 green cardamom pods
- 4 Indian bay leaves or Mediterranean bay leaves
- 2 whole star anise cloves
- 1 cup finely chopped red onion
- 2 cups basmati rice, rinsed and drained
- 3 cups hot water
- 1 cup coconut milk
- 1 teaspoon kosher salt

1 In a large bowl, mix the shrimp, turmeric, lime juice, and ginger-garlic paste and toss to combine. Cover and refrigerate the shrimp while you prepare the masala paste in step 2 and start the pilaf.

2 In a blender, combine the coconut, tomato purée, chiles, chili powder, cilantro, garlic, ginger, and 2 tablespoons of water and purée until smooth, about 1 minute. Set aside.

3 In a heavy saucepan, heat the oil over medium-high heat until it's shimmering. Add the cloves, cinnamon, cardamom, bay leaves, and star anise. Cook, stirring, until fragrant, about 1 minute. Add the onion and cook, stirring, until it is softened and just beginning to brown, about 3 minutes.

4 Add the marinated shrimp and cook, stirring, until fragrant, about 1 minute. Add the masala paste from the blender and mix well to distribute the paste and coat the shrimp. Stir vigorously until the mixture is well blended and the oil starts to separate from the sauce, about 2 minutes.

5 Add the rice to the pan and stir gently until the spice mixture coats the grains. Add the hot water, coconut milk, and salt. Cover the pan, and bring the liquid to a boil over high heat. Reduce the heat to medium-low, remove the lid, and let the mixture cook without stirring until the rice is tender and the liquid has been absorbed, about 15 minutes.

6 Serve immediately with fried poppadums (see Ingredient Tip) and Cooling Yogurt and Vegetable Salad (page 104).

Ingredient Tip: Poppadums are thin, dehydrated dough sheets that are fried in oil until they are crisp. They can be made with a variety of flours, including rice, lentil, potato, tapioca, and chickpea. Indian people typically buy them dehydrated so they don't have to make them from scratch. You can find fried poppadums at Indian grocery stores and online.

PLAIN NAAN

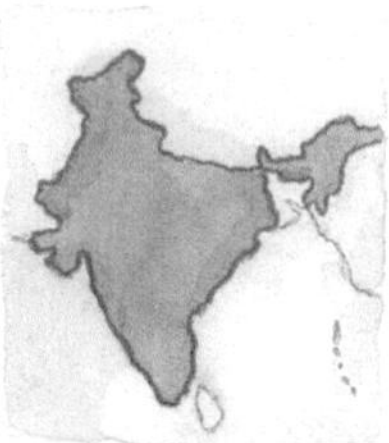

ALL INDIA

VEGETARIAN
EGG-FREE
PEANUT-FREE
SOY-FREE
ALLIUM-FREE

MAKES 10 TO 12 NAANS ◆ PREP TIME: 10 MINUTES, PLUS 2 HOURS TO RISE ◆ COOK TIME: 3 TO 5 MINUTES PER NAAN *Naan is a leavened Indian flatbread that is usually made in a tandoor or clay oven. It is especially popular in North India but is now made across the country. This is a basic naan recipe adapted for the stove top. It uses all-purpose flour, but you can use half white flour and half whole-wheat flour for a healthier result.*

2 teaspoons sugar
¾ cup warm water (not hot)
½ teaspoon active dry yeast
3 cups all-purpose flour (plus extra for rolling)
Pinch kosher salt
1½ tablespoons plain yogurt
4 tablespoons melted ghee or vegetable oil, plus more for cooking and serving

1 In a small bowl, dissolve the sugar in the water. Stir in the yeast and set the bowl aside in a warm part of the kitchen for about 15 minutes, until the mixture is cloudy and a bit bubbly.

2 In a large mixing bowl, stir together the flour and salt. Stir the yogurt into the foamy yeast mixture, then pour the yogurt-yeast mixture into the bowl with the flour, along with the ghee. Stir until a sticky dough forms, then turn the dough out onto a clean work surface and knead it until it's smooth and less sticky. If the dough is not coming together, add more water, 1 tablespoon at a time, kneading between each addition. Cover the dough with a damp kitchen towel and allow it to rise in a warm spot for at least 1½ hours.

3 When the dough has doubled in size, punch it down and form it into 10 to 12 small balls. Cover these with a damp kitchen towel and let them rise again for 15 to 20 minutes.

4 Heat a griddle or tava over medium heat. As the pan heats, lightly dust a clean work surface with flour and roll out each ball into a 6-inch disk.

5 Brush some oil on one side of a disk and place that side onto the hot pan. Cook until brown spots appear on the bottom. (Lift the naan slightly to check this.) Then brush some oil on the top and turn over the naan. Cook until the other side is lightly browned and crisp.

6 Set the pan on another burner. If you have a gas stove, hold the naan with tongs and expose the naan to the open flame on each side for about 10 seconds, ensuring the whole side is exposed to the flame. This gives the naan a smoky flavor and slight char. Alternatively, if you have an electric stove, use the oven to broil the naan for 10 to 30 seconds per side. Remove the finished naan to a plate and brush it with additional ghee before serving.

7 Repeat until all the naans are cooked.

Serving Tip: Naans are best eaten warm, straight off the stove. They tend to become very chewy when cold.

AMRITSARI FLATBREAD

Kulcha

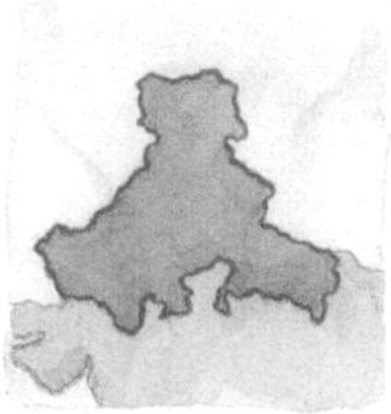

NORTH INDIA

VEGETARIAN
EGG-FREE
PEANUT-FREE
SOY-FREE
ALLIUM-FREE

MAKES 8 TO 10 FLATBREADS ◆ PREP TIME: 20 MINUTES, PLUS 2 HOURS TO RISE ◆ COOK TIME: 30 MINUTES *This simple Indian flatbread is famous in North India, with the best ones coming out of the kitchens of Amritsar in Punjab. I remember going to a dhaaba (a roadside eatery) there for a breakfast of kulchas with stewed chickpeas and tangy onion salad. You can serve these kulchas in any meal that calls for Indian flatbreads like roti or naan.*

- 2½ cups all-purpose flour, plus more for dusting
- 1 teaspoon kosher salt
- 2 teaspoons sugar
- ½ teaspoon baking powder
- ¼ teaspoon baking soda
- 4 tablespoons plain yogurt
- 3 tablespoons melted ghee or vegetable oil
- ¾ cup water, at room temperature
- 1 tablespoon nigella seeds
- 1 tablespoon white sesame seeds or a mix of black and white

1 In a large bowl, mix together the flour, salt, sugar, baking powder, and baking soda. Make a well in the center and add the yogurt, ghee, and water.

2 Using your fingers, mix the flour into the liquids, and when all the liquid is combined, transfer the mixture to a clean work surface and knead it until a soft, smooth dough forms. Cover the dough with a damp kitchen towel and allow it to rise in a warm spot for 2 hours.

3 Divide the dough into 8 to 10 balls. In a small bowl, mix the nigella seeds and sesame seeds. Sprinkle some of this mixture over each ball of dough.

4 Heat a cast-iron skillet or tava over medium-high heat. Using a rolling pin, flatten each ball of dough into a 5- to 6-inch disk. Place one disk in the hot skillet and cook for 30 to 40 seconds. Using a pastry brush, apply a little ghee to the bread, flip it over with a spatula, and then brush the other side with more ghee.

5 Flip two to three more times, basting with ghee each time, until the bread is fully cooked through and is lightly charred in spots on both sides. Repeat the process with the rest of the dough pieces. Serve hot with another brush of ghee and some Punjabi Chickpea Curry (page 152) on the side.

Serving Tip: When the kulchas are finished cooking, keep them warm by stashing them in a packet made of aluminum foil or in a container with a lid.

DEEP-FRIED BREAD

Bhatura

NORTH INDIA

VEGETARIAN
EGG-FREE
PEANUT-FREE
SOY-FREE
ALLIUM-FREE

MAKES ABOUT 10 ◆ PREP TIME: 20 MINUTES, PLUS 2 HOURS TO RISE ◆ COOK TIME: 10 MINUTES *Bhaturas are commonly made in the north of the country and eaten with lentils and chickpea curries as a hearty meal. Since they are leavened and deep fried, they are puffed up into spheres when they emerge from the hot oil.*

2 cups all-purpose flour
1 teaspoon baking soda
Kosher salt
2 tablespoons fine semolina flour (rava)
1 teaspoon sugar
1 cup plain yogurt
1 teaspoon carom seeds (optional)
1 tablespoon water
Vegetable oil, for deep frying

1 In a mixing bowl, sift together the flour, baking soda, and a pinch of salt. Add the semolina flour, sugar, yogurt, carom seeds (if using), and water. Mix together and then knead into a smooth dough. Add more water if needed. Cover the dough with a damp cloth and set aside in a warm place for 2 hours.

2 In a heavy saucepan, heat a couple of inches of oil for deep frying until the oil is shimmering. Divide the dough into 10 to 12 small balls and keep them covered with a damp cloth while you roll each one out. Using a rolling pin, roll each ball into a 4- to 5-inch round or oblong bread and gently add to the hot oil.

3 With the back of a slotted spoon, apply light pressure on the bhatura in the hot oil so that it puffs up. Turn and fry evenly on both sides. Remove and drain on paper towels. Repeat with the rest of the balls. Serve hot.

Serving Tip: These bhaturas from Himachal are great to eat on a cold or rainy day with a piping hot bowl of Punjabi Chickpea Curry (page 152) as a hearty breakfast.

EASY RICE AND LENTIL CRÊPES

Dosas

SOUTH INDIA

VEGAN
GLUTEN-FREE
PEANUT-FREE
SOY-FREE
ALLIUM-FREE

SERVES 4 ♦ PREP TIME: 10 MINUTES, PLUS OVERNIGHT TO RISE ♦ COOK TIME: 15 MINUTES *The dosa is a fermented rice pancake or crêpe that is a staple in South India. My easy dosa version from Kerala does away with soaking and grinding raw rice and lentils by using flour versions of both. This reduces the whole process by at least 4 to 5 hours.*

1½ cups rice flour
¾ cup husked black lentil flour (urad dal)
2½ cups water, plus more as required
Kosher salt
1 teaspoon oil, divided

1 In a large bowl, mix the rice and lentil flours. Add the water and mix well so that there are no lumps and the batter is smooth, like a thick, pourable pancake batter. Pour this batter into another clean bowl, cover with a damp cloth, and let it rise overnight in a warm location.

2 The next day, add a dash of salt to the batter and mix well.

3 Heat ½ teaspoon oil in a cast-iron skillet or tava over medium-high heat. Pour in a ladle full of batter and use the back of the ladle to smear the batter across the bottom of the pan. Try to get an even, thin layer of batter.

4 Cook for 1 minute and drizzle ½ teaspoon of oil around the sides of the pan so the dosa will crisp up and cook evenly. Gently lift the dosa and check if the underside is lightly browned. When it is browned, flip the dosa and cook the other side until browned. Repeat with the rest of the batter.

5 Serve immediately with Coconut Chutney (page 114) and hot coffee or tea.

Cooking Tip: Store the batter in the refrigerator for up to 5 days after it has risen. Remove the bowl about 10 minutes before cooking to bring the batter to room temperature.

QUICK-STEAMED SEMOLINA BUNS

Rava Idli

SOUTH INDIA

VEGETARIAN
EGG-FREE
PEANUT-FREE
SOY-FREE
ALLIUM-FREE

SERVES 2 TO 3 ◆ PREP TIME: 15 MINUTES, PLUS 15 MINUTES TO REST ◆ COOK TIME: 20 MINUTES *Steamed buns and crêpes form a large part of the South Indian diet. While they are commonly made using ground rice and lentils that have to be fermented overnight, this quick semolina version from Karnataka is ready to steam in a matter of minutes. To up the nutritional content, consider adding grated or finely sliced vegetables and herbs.*

- 1 tablespoon vegetable oil
- 1 teaspoon black mustard seeds
- Pinch asafetida
- 2 teaspoons split husked black lentils (urad dal)
- 6 cashews, chopped coarsely (optional)
- 1 (1-inch) piece fresh ginger, finely chopped (optional)
- 1 green chile, seeded and finely chopped
- 10 curry leaves (optional)
- 1 cup semolina (rava)
- 1 cup plain yogurt
- 2 tablespoons chopped cilantro leaves
- 1 medium carrot, grated (optional)
- ¼ teaspoon baking soda
- Kosher salt
- 2 tablespoons water
- Unsalted butter or ghee, for greasing the ramekins

1 Heat the oil in a medium skillet over medium heat until it begins to shimmer. Add the mustard seeds and stand back. When they crackle, add a pinch of asafetida and the lentils, stirring frequently. When the lentils brown slightly, after 2 to 3 minutes, add the cashews (if using) and ginger (if using), chile, and curry leaves (if using). Stand back, as the curry leaves may crackle in the oil.

2 Turn the heat to medium-low, add the semolina, and roast it for a few minutes. Do not allow it to change color or burn, but make sure it is coated with the oil and becomes slightly fragrant. Turn the heat off, transfer the mixture to a bowl, and allow it to cool completely.

3 When the semolina mixture is cool, add the yogurt, cilantro, carrot (if using), baking soda, and season with salt. Gradually add a couple of tablespoons of water and mix it well until there are no lumps. The batter should be similar to a thick waffle batter—not too thin, not too thick. Adjust the water accordingly and let the batter rest 15 minutes.

4 Pour 2 inches of water in a large saucepan, and set a large bamboo steamer or metal steamer basket inside. Grease six individual steel ramekins or molds with butter, and place them on a single plate that you can fit into the steamer. Pour the batter into the molds or ramekins, leaving about ¾ inch at the top of each to give the buns room to rise. Place them in the steamer, cover, and steam over medium-high heat for 10 to 15 minutes or until the buns are set and begin to pull away from the sides.

5 Turn off the heat, open the lid, and allow the buns to air-dry for 5 minutes before removing. Serve them warm with Coconut Chutney (page 114), Cilantro and Mint Chutney (page 110), and some hot coffee and tea.

Did You Know? In India, steamed breads are made in a stack of stainless steel trays called an idli steamer. As the water simmers, the steam cooks the idlis in the trays.

GOAN FERMENTED STEAMED BUNS

Sannas

WEST AND CENTRAL INDIA

VEGAN
GLUTEN-FREE
PEANUT-FREE
SOY-FREE
ALLIUM-FREE

MAKES 10 TO 12 BUNS ◆ PREP TIME: 40 MINUTES, PLUS OVERNIGHT TO SOAK AND 2 HOURS TO RISE ◆ COOK TIME: 15 MINUTES *Sanna is the go-to bread for scooping up the tangy flavors of classic Indian-Catholic cuisine. It is a steamed bun that is traditionally fermented with toddy—a locally brewed liquor made from the date palm—but I use yeast instead. Sannas are slightly sweet and have a distinct tanginess that pairs well with the spicy curries of the region.*

- 2 cups white rice
- 1 tablespoon fresh yeast or 1½ tablespoons dry activated yeast
- 3½ tablespoons sugar, divided
- ½ cup warm water
- 1 cup fresh or frozen shredded coconut
- 1½ teaspoons kosher salt
- Vegetable oil, for greasing

1 Wash the rice, place it in a large bowl, and pour in enough cold water to cover it by at least 1 inch. Cover the bowl and let the rice soak overnight at room temperature.

2 The next day, in a small bowl, whisk together the yeast, ½ tablespoon of sugar, and the warm water. Cover and set aside in a warm spot until the mixture is bubbly and frothy, about 20 minutes.

3 Drain the rice and transfer it to a blender or spice grinder along with the coconut and remaining 3 tablespoons of sugar, working in batches if necessary. Process the mixture until it resembles a very fine, pourable paste. If the paste is too thick, add a few tablespoons of water at a time, ensuring that you do not end up with a runny liquid. The paste should be fine with almost no grittiness from the rice or coconut. Transfer the mixture to a large bowl.

4 Check the yeast: If it is bubbling and frothy, add it to the rice mixture. If it is not, wait until it is, and continue. Add the salt and mix well. Cover and allow the mixture to rise in a warm place for about 2 hours. After 2 hours, it should have expanded in size and will have some air bubbles on the top.

5 Pour 2 inches of water in a large saucepan and set a large bamboo steamer or metal steamer basket inside. Grease 10 to 12 individual steel ramekins or molds with oil and place them on a single plate that you can fit into the steamer (or work in batches if you don't have a large enough steamer). Pour the batter into the molds or ramekins, leaving about ¾ inch at the top of each to give the buns room to rise. Place them in the steamer, cover, and steam over medium-high heat for 10 to 15 minutes, or until the buns are firm and glossy.

Serving Tip: If you need to reheat the sannas in the microwave, always put them in a covered dish and leave it closed for a minute after heating. The steam will keep them soft.

5

SALADS, CHUTNEYS, AND PICKLES

COOLING YOGURT AND VEGETABLE SALAD

Raita

ALL INDIA

VEGETARIAN
EGG-FREE
GLUTEN-FREE
PEANUT-FREE
SOY-FREE

SERVES 2 • PREP TIME: 15 MINUTES *This yogurt-based salad cools the body internally and adds a mellow balance to the spice of an Indian meal. Raitas can be sweet or savory, but the best part about them is their versatility: Popular ingredients range from fruits and vegetables to herbs and crunchy deep-fried balls (boondi).*

- 1½ cups plain yogurt
- 1 teaspoon sugar
- ½ teaspoon Roasted Cumin Powder (page 42), plus garnish for serving
- ¼ teaspoon black salt or rock salt (optional)
- Kosher salt
- 1 cucumber, peeled and chopped
- 1 tomato, chopped
- 1 scallion or small red onion, finely chopped (optional)
- 1 tablespoon chopped mint leaves
- 1 tablespoon chopped cilantro leaves
- 1 green chile, seeded and finely chopped

1 In a small bowl, whisk the yogurt until smooth. Add the sugar, cumin powder, and black salt (if using). Season with salt and mix well.

2 Mix in the cucumber, tomato, scallion (if using), mint, cilantro, and chile. Serve with a light garnish of cumin powder on top.

To make other raitas

For pineapple/pomegranate raita, leave out the kosher salt, vegetables, and herbs. Add chopped pineapple pieces or pomegranate seeds and a few chopped mint leaves to the yogurt, and adjust the seasonings. Use the rock salt and a light dusting of cumin powder as garnish.

For cucumber and roasted peanut raita, leave out the onion, tomato, and mint. Add coarsely crushed roasted peanuts instead.

Substitution Tip: Make it vegan by using cashew yogurt. To mimic the tanginess of the yogurt, add a teaspoon of lime juice and follow the rest of the recipe above.

TANGY MIXED-VEGETABLE SALAD

Parsi Kachumbar

WEST AND CENTRAL INDIA

VEGAN
GLUTEN-FREE
PEANUT-FREE
SOY-FREE

SERVES 2 ◆ PREP TIME: 20 MINUTES *Kachumbar is a fresh, finely chopped vegetable salad usually tossed with citrus dressing. This Parsi recipe from Maharashtra is bold in its use of vinegar and adds a punchy burst of flavor to any meal. I personally love eating this with Parsi dhansaak, a lentil and lamb stew, and brown rice on a Sunday, and then submitting to a long siesta.*

- 1 large tomato, finely chopped, divided
- 1 small red onion, finely diced, divided
- 1 green chile, seeded and chopped, divided
- 1 tablespoon finely chopped cilantro leaves and stems, separated
- 1½ teaspoons finely chopped mint leaves
- 1 teaspoon sugar
- ½ teaspoon kosher salt
- 1½ teaspoons palm vinegar, coconut vinegar, or white vinegar
- 1 teaspoon freshly squeezed lime juice (optional)
- 1 medium cucumber, seeded and diced

1 In a mortar and pestle, add half the tomato, 1 teaspoon of the onion, half the chile, the cilantro stems, mint, sugar, salt, vinegar, and lime juice (if using). Gently pound to blend the flavors. Check the seasonings and add salt if needed.

2 In another bowl, add the remaining tomato, onion, chile, cilantro, and cucumber, and mix. Pour the pounded dressing over the vegetables and serve chilled.

Cooking Tip: You can make this salad the night before for an easy side dish. The vinegar and sugar mature and make the vegetables taste even better when left overnight.

GOAN RUSSIAN SALAD

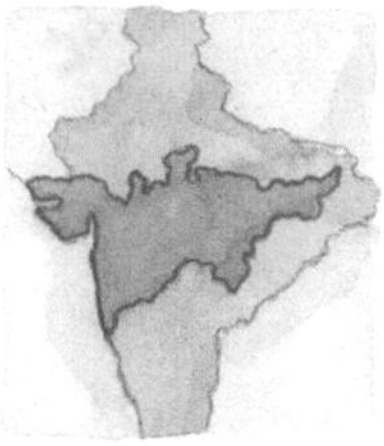

WEST AND CENTRAL INDIA

DAIRY-FREE
GLUTEN-FREE
PEANUT-FREE
SOY-FREE

SERVES 4 TO 6 ♦ PREP TIME: 20 MINUTES, PLUS 1 HOUR TO CHILL *A Goan Catholic wedding buffet is incomplete without this much-loved Russian Salad, though no one knows where it got its name. In this version, I love the interplay of sweet pineapple, crispy cucumber, and celery, as well as the mild heat of the hot sauce added to the mayonnaise. It's almost a meal in itself.*

1 medium cucumber, seeded and diced
1 large tomato, seeded and chopped
1 cup boiled, peeled, and chopped potato
1 tablespoon chopped celery
2 tablespoons chopped scallions, green parts only
½ cup chopped pineapple
½ cup boiled green peas
1 small bell pepper (any color), seeded and chopped
½ cup cooked, diced chicken or ham
1 hardboiled egg, finely chopped
½ cup boiled and chopped small shrimp (optional)
1 cup mayonnaise
1 tablespoon tomato ketchup
Dash Tabasco sauce
1 teaspoon freshly ground black pepper
Kosher salt

1 In a large bowl, mix together all the ingredients and season with salt; cover and chill for at least 1 hour before serving.

2 Serve cold.

Serving Tip: This salad is a lovely accompaniment to a Goan meal of Pork Vindaloo (page 176) and Goan Fermented Steamed Buns (page 100).

MANIPURI MIXED-VEGETABLE SALAD

Singju

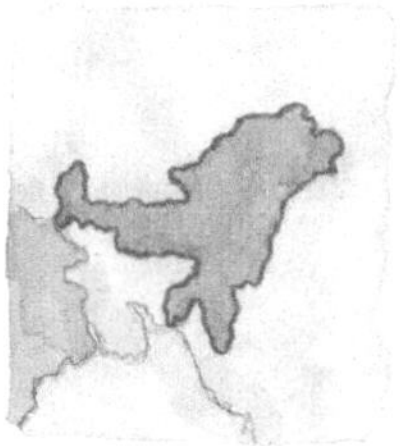

NORTHEAST INDIA

GLUTEN-FREE
PEANUT-FREE
SOY-FREE
ALLIUM-FREE

SERVES 2 ♦ PREP TIME: 20 MINUTES ♦ COOK TIME: 5 MINUTES *Manipur and its neighboring states in Northeast India have cuisine brimming with fresh vegetables, chiles, and fermented fish. This salad traditionally uses a fresh hot pepper called the king chile, which is extremely spicy and difficult to find, so in my version I use a Thai chile instead. If you want to reduce the heat, remove the chile's seeds before using.*

- 1 tablespoon black sesame seeds
- 1 tablespoon chickpea flour
- 1 whole green Thai chile
- ½ teaspoon Asian fish sauce or fish paste
- Kosher salt
- 3 tablespoons fresh blanched peas
- ½ cup shredded cabbage
- ½ cup shredded raw green papaya

1 On a skillet or tava over medium heat, dry roast the sesame seeds for a few seconds till aromatic and set them aside to cool. When they are cool, grind them to a powder in a spice grinder.

2 In the same skillet, dry roast the chickpea flour for a few seconds on low heat, and transfer it to a medium bowl.

3 In the same skillet, dry roast the chile over medium-high heat until the skin blackens a bit, and then transfer it to a mortar and pestle. Pour in ¼ cup of water and grind the chile until it forms a loose paste.

4 To the bowl with the chickpea flour, add the fish sauce, chile mixture, and sesame seed powder. Mix well. Taste and season with salt to make a dressing.

5 Arrange the peas, shredded cabbage, and papaya in a serving bowl. Pour the dressing over the vegetables; toss well and serve.

Ingredients Tip: This salad is sometimes made using dried white peas (ragda vatana) instead of blanched green peas. Soak the dried white peas for at least 6 hours, then boil until tender, 30 to 40 minutes.

SESAME SEED CHUTNEY

Til ki Chetni

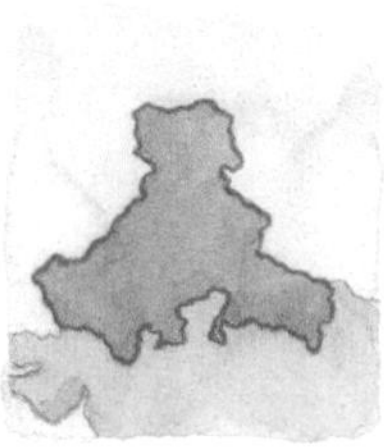

NORTH INDIA

VEGETARIAN
EGG-FREE
GLUTEN-FREE
PEANUT-FREE
SOY-FREE

MAKES ABOUT ½ CUP ♦ PREP TIME: 10 MINUTES ♦ COOK TIME: 5 MINUTES

In India's Himalayan states, especially Uttarakhand, the food of the region is closely tied to the seasons. During winter, til ki chetni is enjoyed in almost every home because of its warming qualities and bright flavor. When it's bitter cold outside, a few spoonfuls of this chutney with dal and rice is just the thing to put a warm smile on your face.

3 tablespoons white sesame seeds
½ cup chopped cilantro leaves
3 garlic cloves, peeled
1 to 2 green chiles
3 tablespoons plain yogurt or freshly squeezed lime juice
½ teaspoon sugar (optional)
Kosher salt

1 In a cast-iron skillet or tava over low heat, roast the sesame seeds for about 2 minutes, taking care not to burn them. Remove and cool the seeds on a plate. Transfer to a mortar and pestle or spice grinder and grind finely.

2 Add the cilantro, garlic, and chiles and continue grinding. Add the yogurt, and sugar (if using). Grind to a fine paste. Season with salt.

3 Serve immediately as a dip with Plain Naan (page 92), or refrigerate for up to 1 day if using yogurt and 2 to 3 days if using only lime.

Substitution Tip: Make this chutney allium-free by omitting the garlic and adding ¼ teaspoon asafetida.

SWEET AND SOUR TAMARIND CHUTNEY

Imli ki Chutney

ALL INDIA

MAKES ABOUT 1½ CUPS ♦ PREP TIME: 15 MINUTES *This classic sweet and sour condiment is served with a variety of Indian snacks throughout the country and makes a special appearance during the Hindu festival of Navratri, when people observe fasts and eat only certain foods. Imli ki chutney balances spiciness with the mellow sweetness of dates and jaggery and the tartness of tamarind. You can adjust the spiciness while preparing it, and it will store well in the refrigerator for about a month.*

FESTIVAL FOOD

VEGAN
GLUTEN-FREE
PEANUT-FREE
SOY-FREE
ALLIUM-FREE

- ½ cup pitted dates
- 1 tablespoon raisins (optional)
- ½ cup tamarind paste
- 2 tablespoons powdered, or grated, jaggery or sugar
- 1 teaspoon Roasted Cumin Powder (page 42)
- ½ teaspoon ground coriander
- 1 teaspoon black salt or rock salt
- ½ to 1 teaspoon red chili powder
- 1 teaspoon chaat masala (optional)
- Water
- Kosher salt

1 Place the dates and raisins (if using) in a small bowl and pour in enough warm water to cover them. Let them soak for about 10 minutes. When they are soft, add the tamarind paste, then transfer the mixture to a blender or spice grinder and process until smooth.

2 Add the jaggery, cumin powder, coriander, rock salt, chili powder, and chaat masala (if using) to the blender or grinder. Process until smooth, adding a little water at a time until the chutney reaches your desired consistency. Season with kosher salt.

3 Serve as a dipping sauce or with Crispy Spiced-Potato Snack (page 54), or transfer the chutney to an airtight container and refrigerate for up to 3 weeks.

Cooking Tip: If you add more water to make a thinner chutney, make sure to check the seasonings, as you might need to add more salt, cumin, and chili powder before serving.

CILANTRO AND MINT CHUTNEY

Hari Chutney

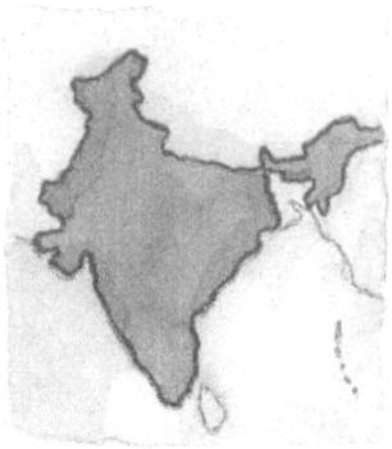

ALL INDIA

VEGAN
GLUTEN-FREE
PEANUT-FREE
SOY-FREE
ALLIUM-FREE

MAKES ABOUT 1 CUP ♦ PREP TIME: 10 MINUTES *This chutney is an important component of chaat snacks, but it can also be used as a delicious spread for sandwiches or a filling for dumplings. I keep a small bowl of this handy in my refrigerator for use in curry bases, marinades, yogurt dips, and even in tiny quantities as a flavoring for oil and vinegar–based salad dressings.*

- 1 cup cilantro leaves and tender stalks, chopped
- ½ cup mint leaves
- 1 (½-inch) piece fresh ginger (optional)
- 2 to 3 green chiles
- 1 teaspoon sugar
- 1½ teaspoons freshly squeezed lime juice
- ½ teaspoon black salt or rock salt
- 1 teaspoon Roasted Cumin Powder (page 42)
- 1 teaspoon chaat masala (optional)
- Kosher salt

1 In a blender, combine the cilantro, mint, ginger (if using), chiles, sugar, lime juice, black salt, cumin powder, and chaat masala (if using). Process until smooth, adding a bit of water to aid in the grinding. Season with salt.

2 Check the spice level and seasoning. There should be a balanced mix of sweet, salty, and spicy in this chutney.

3 Serve with an Indian snack, or store refrigerated for up to 3 days in an airtight container.

Cooking Tip: You can also add a clove of garlic to this chutney. It makes for a nice flavor variation and is tastier when using this chutney as a sandwich spread.

TANGY-SWEET MANGO CHUTNEY

Aam Chunda

WEST AND CENTRAL INDIA

VEGAN
PEANUT-FREE
SOY-FREE
ALLIUM-FREE

MAKES ABOUT 2 CUPS • PREP TIME: 15 MINUTES • COOK TIME: 20 TO 25 MINUTES

During mango season in India, the raw, unripened fruits are the first to hit the markets, and before they can develop their natural sugars, they are pickled, preserved, and bottled in tangy-sweet chutneys like this one. It is a popular dish in Gujarat, where there's a touch of sweetness in almost every dish.

- 1¼ cups large raw green mangoes, peeled, pitted, and grated on a box grater
- 1½ cups sugar
- 1 teaspoon turmeric powder
- Kosher salt
- 1 whole red or green chile (optional)
- 1 teaspoon red chili powder
- ½ teaspoon Roasted Cumin Powder (page 42)

1 In a medium saucepan, add the grated mango, sugar, and turmeric. Season with salt. Place on medium-low heat and stir to mix. Turn the heat to low and keep stirring. The sugar will begin to melt, and water will leech out of the mangoes. Add the whole chile (if using).

2 Cook on low for about 15 minutes, until the mixture starts to thicken and the sugar becomes syrupy and has a thread-like consistency. When it has the consistency of jam, turn off the heat.

3 Add the chili powder and cumin powder. Stir to mix thoroughly. Allow it to cool and serve as a condiment to any meal, or have it with Plain Naan (page 92). You can store the remaining chunda in a sterilized glass jar in the refrigerator for up to 2 months.

Serving Tip: Use a separate, dry spoon to serve mango chutney; using a spoon that is also used in other dishes might make this chutney spoil.

DRIED-SHRIMP CHUTNEY

Galmbyachi Chetni

SOUTH INDIA

EGG-FREE
DAIRY-FREE
GLUTEN-FREE
PEANUT-FREE
SOY-FREE

MAKES ABOUT 1½ CUPS ♦ PREP TIME: 10 MINUTES ♦ COOK TIME: 20 MINUTES

The monsoon season is eagerly awaited across India, as it irrigates the fields and provides respite from the unforgiving summer heat. One gloomy part of this, however, is that those who live in coastal states are unable to go out and fish. This chutney from Mangalore is served as a pleasant reminder of the bounty of summer during the fish-lean monsoon season. It is a strong, bold condiment packed with dried shrimp, a flavor you either love or hate.

1¾ ounces dried shrimp (jawla)
½ cup fresh, or frozen and thawed, grated coconut
1 teaspoon red chili powder
1 teaspoon ground cumin
¼ teaspoon turmeric powder
1 teaspoon tamarind paste
1½ teaspoons vegetable oil
1 tablespoon finely chopped red onion
Kosher salt

1 Wash the dried shrimp a couple of times, then wrap them in a clean kitchen towel and squeeze them over the sink until they are dry. (Or drain them thoroughly in a colander and pat them dry with a kitchen towel.)

2 Heat a cast-iron skillet or tava over medium heat until hot. Adjust the heat to medium-low, add the shrimp, and dry roast them, stirring frequently, until they develop a slight crispness and become aromatic, 2 to 5 minutes, depending on the amount of water that is left behind in the shrimp. Transfer the shrimp to a plate to cool.

3 In the same skillet over low heat, add the grated coconut and dry roast until the coconut becomes aromatic and is on the verge of turning brown, 7 to 8 minutes. Continue stirring, as the coconut may stick to the skillet; simply scrape it off the pan gently with a wooden spoon and keep stirring the scrapings back into the rest of the roasting coconut. Remove the skillet from the heat and transfer the coconut to the plate with the shrimp to cool.

4 In a spice grinder, mortar and pestle, or blender, mix the chili powder, cumin, turmeric, tamarind paste, and roasted shrimp and coconut. Grind to a coarse, crumbly mixture. The chutney should resemble coarsely grated coconut and shouldn't be too fine. Add about 2 teaspoons of water just to moisten the mix and make the process easier. Transfer this mixture to a bowl.

5 In a small skillet over medium-high heat, heat the oil until it's shimmering, and add the chopped onion. Stir and fry until the onion is golden brown. Turn off the heat and add the onion and any oil left in the skillet to the shrimp and spice mix. Stir and mix well. Season with salt and serve.

Ingredient Tip: Dried shrimp come already peeled and deveined, and are typically rather small. Find them in Asian or Indian grocery stores, or online.

Serving Tip: This chutney is commonly used as an accompaniment to a main fish-based Indian meal. Because of its strong flavors, it is usually served in small quantities.

COCONUT CHUTNEY

Nariyal Chutney

SOUTH INDIA

VEGAN
GLUTEN-FREE
PEANUT-FREE
SOY-FREE
ALLIUM-FREE

MAKES ABOUT 1 CUP ◆ PREP TIME: 10 MINUTES ◆ COOK TIME: 5 MINUTES

This quick and easy chutney from Kerala is a popular condiment served with breakfast dishes like Quick-Steamed Semolina Buns (page 98) and Easy Rice and Lentil Crêpes (page 97). It is a staple chutney in most of South India, and you'll find it almost everywhere you travel. I love the way the tempering of the spices adds a subtle, delicious reminder of the South.

1 cup fresh, or frozen and thawed, grated coconut
1½ teaspoons tamarind paste
2 to 3 tablespoons water
Kosher salt
1½ tablespoons coconut or vegetable oil
2 dried red chiles, such as Kashmiri chiles, broken in half or thirds
2 teaspoons black mustard seeds
2 teaspoons husked black lentils (urad dal)
10 to 12 curry leaves (optional)

1 Using a blender, spice grinder, or mortar and pestle, grind the coconut and tamarind until smooth. Add 2 to 3 tablespoons of water and grind again. Season with salt and mix well. Transfer to a serving bowl.

2 In a small skillet, heat the oil over medium heat until it's shimmering. Turn the heat to medium-low. Add the chiles and stir briefly until fragrant, 20 to 30 seconds. In quick succession, add the mustard seeds, wait until they pop, then stir in the lentils and cook, stirring constantly, until they turn light brown. Add the curry leaves (if using), and stand back, allowing them to splatter. Mix well, remove the skillet from the heat, and pour this flavored oil immediately over the coconut chutney in the bowl.

3 Stir just once, so that some of the flavored oil is mixed through and some is still visible as a garnish on the top of the chutney. Serve immediately with Quick-Steamed Semolina Buns (page 98) or Easy Rice and Lentil Crêpes (page 97).

Substitution Tip: If you cannot find dried red chiles, you can use green chiles in the same quantity. You can also add about 1 teaspoon finely sliced ginger to the oil for a slightly different flavor.

Ingredient Tip: This chutney doesn't have a long shelf life. The fresh coconut will go rancid quickly, so it's best eaten right when you make it.

ROASTED GREEN CHILE CHUTNEY

Hmarcha Rawt

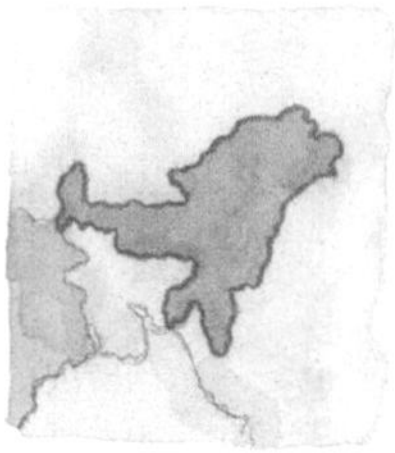

NORTHEAST INDIA

VEGAN
GLUTEN-FREE
PEANUT-FREE
SOY-FREE

MAKES ¼ TO ½ CUP ◆ PREP TIME: 5 MINUTES ◆ COOK TIME: 5 MINUTES

While the cuisine of Northeast India is largely mild, this area is famous for some of the hottest chiles in the world, which make their way into very hot chile chutneys and accompaniments. This chutney from Mizoram is not for the faint of heart, but I find that it's a rather enjoyable adventure for the taste buds.

10 green chiles
Kosher salt
1 (1-inch) piece fresh ginger, finely chopped
2 tablespoons very finely chopped red onion

1 Heat a cast-iron skillet or tava over medium heat. When hot, add the whole chiles and dry roast until most of the skin is speckled black, about 5 minutes, turning the chiles for even blackening. Transfer to a plate to cool. Remove and discard the stems from the chiles.

2 Using a mortar and pestle or spice grinder, grind the chiles, salt, and ginger until mixed but not fine; the finished chutney should be quite chunky. Transfer to a bowl and add the onion.

3 Serve as a side to a main meal.

Cooking Tip: If finely chopping an onion proves daunting, just coarsely chop the onion and add it to the mortar and pestle after you've ground the chile and ginger a bit. Pulse or pound until just chunky.

SZECHUAN CHUTNEY

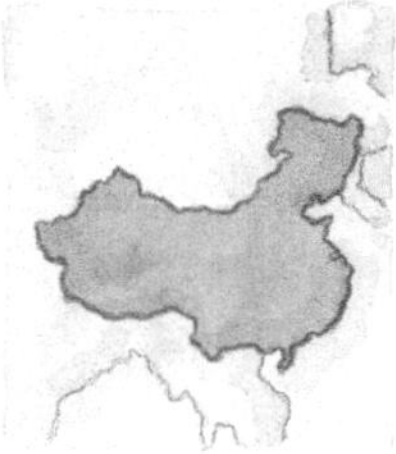

INDIAN-CHINESE

VEGAN
GLUTEN-FREE
PEANUT-FREE

MAKES ABOUT 1½ CUPS ◆ PREP TIME: 15 MINUTES, PLUS 30 MINUTES TO SOAK ◆ COOK TIME: 15 MINUTES *Indian-Chinese food is a cuisine unto itself. This hybrid may have started out with authentic Chinese influences during the time of the spice and silk trade routes, but it has now become a mainstream sub-cuisine of India. Szechuan chutney is hot, garlicky, slightly sweet, and has a vibrant red hue that adds drama to any Indian-Chinese meal.*

1 cup dried red chiles
½ cup vegetable oil
5 tablespoons minced garlic
2 tablespoons minced fresh ginger
1 teaspoon light or dark soy sauce
1 tablespoon tomato ketchup
½ teaspoon sugar
Kosher salt

1 In a small saucepan, boil 1 cup of water. Turn off the heat and add the chiles. Soak the chiles for at least 30 minutes to soften. Drain the water and grind the chiles in a spice grinder or mortar and pestle until smooth.

2 In a heavy saucepan, wok, or kadhai, heat the oil over medium heat until it's shimmering. Add the garlic and ginger and sauté for 1 minute, until aromatic, taking care not to brown or burn them. Add the red chili paste, soy sauce, ketchup, and sugar, and cook over medium heat until the sauce thickens and the oil floats to the surface. Season with salt. Let the chutney come to room temperature before serving.

3 Store the chutney in an airtight container in the refrigerator for up to 2 weeks.

Serving Tip: Serve with Indian or Indian-Chinese snacks, or in the preparation of Szechuan Fried Basmati Rice (page 82).

MANGO PICKLES

Maangaiy Urukaiy

SOUTH INDIA

VEGAN
GLUTEN-FREE
PEANUT-FREE
SOY-FREE

MAKES ABOUT ½ TO 1 POUND ◆ PREP TIME: 20 MINUTES, PLUS 2 HOURS TO DRY ◆ COOK TIME: 30 MINUTES ◆ PICKLING TIME: 2 WEEKS TO 1 MONTH ◆ SHELF LIFE: 1 YEAR *There are countless variations of mango pickles made in each state and household throughout India. None of them taste the same, and family recipes are closely guarded secrets. This particular mango pickle, from the former French colony of Pondicherry, is sweet, hot, and tangy, and it makes almost any meal spring to life.*

- 1 large green mango
- ½ teaspoon fenugreek seeds
- 3½ teaspoons black mustard seeds, divided
- 2 teaspoons cumin seeds
- ½ cup sesame oil
- 1 (2-inch) piece fresh ginger, finely chopped
- 15 to 20 garlic cloves, peeled
- 4 green chiles, finely chopped
- ½ teaspoon asafetida
- ½ teaspoon turmeric powder
- 3 to 4 tablespoons red chili powder
- 15 curry leaves (optional)
- 2 tablespoons palm vinegar, coconut vinegar, or white vinegar
- 1 tablespoon kosher salt
- 1 tablespoon sugar

1 Wash and dry the mango thoroughly with a cloth and leave it in the sun for 1 hour. Chop the mango into small, slender pieces without peeling, spread them out on a plate or baking sheet, and leave them in the sun to dry for at least 1 more hour.

2 In a dry skillet over medium heat, roast the fenugreek seeds, 2 teaspoons of mustard seeds, and the cumin seeds. Remove the skillet from the heat and transfer the seeds to a plate to cool. When they are cool, transfer the seeds to a mortar and pestle or spice grinder and grind them to a fine powder. Set aside.

3 In a heavy saucepan, wok, or kadhai, heat the oil over low heat, taking care not to let it smoke. Add the remaining 1½ teaspoons mustard seeds and let them crackle. Add the ginger, garlic, and chiles, and stir until fragrant, 1 or 2 minutes, taking care not to brown any of the ingredients.

4 Add the asafetida, turmeric, and chili powder, stirring continuously for about 10 seconds, as these powders all burn easily. Add the curry leaves (if using) and stir until they become aromatic, about 10 more seconds. Add the dried mango pieces, vinegar, salt, and sugar, increase the heat to medium, and bring the mixture to a gentle boil. Remove the pan from the heat.

5 Add the spice powder to the mango mixture. Transfer the mixture to a glass or ceramic jar with a lid and seal. Shake the jar gently to ensure that the top of the mixture is covered in oil. If not, heat a little additional oil and add it to the jar. This forms a seal that protects the pickles from spoiling. Leave the jar to rest uncovered on the counter until the pickles come to room temperature. Then screw on the lid and place the jar in a warm, dry location for 15 days to 1 month.

Ingredient Tip: Sometimes the mangoes may be firm even after waiting for a couple of weeks. Just leave the pickles to mature for more days or weeks, and this will be resolved.

Cooking Tip: When serving, remove the amount needed from the jar and place it in a serving bowl. Never put any remaining pickles back into the main jar, as this tends to spoil the pickles.

GOAN-STYLE DRY PRAWN PICKLES

Goan Balchao

WEST AND CENTRAL INDIA

EGG-FREE
DAIRY-FREE
GLUTEN-FREE
PEANUT-FREE
SOY-FREE

MAKES ABOUT 1 POUND ◆ PREP TIME: 10 MINUTES, PLUS 4 HOURS TO SOAK SHRIMP ◆ COOK TIME: 30 TO 40 MINUTES ◆ PICKLING TIME: 2 WEEKS TO 1 MONTH ◆ SHELF LIFE: 1 YEAR *Balchao is a famous seafood pickle from the palm-fringed beaches of Goa. The dish is heavily influenced by the Portuguese, who ruled here decades ago, and it makes liberal use of chili and vinegar. This dish stands out for its wonderfully paired tangy, spicy, and hot combination. It is made with dried tiny shrimp and set aside to be used during the monsoon, when fishing stops. The pungent smell of this pickle is craved by Goans the world over.*

- 7 ounces tiny dried shrimp
- 1 cup plus 2 tablespoons palm vinegar, coconut vinegar, or white vinegar, divided
- ¾ ounce dried red chiles, such as Kashmiri chiles
- 3 tablespoons fresh ginger, coarsely chopped
- 3 tablespoons garlic, coarsely chopped
- ¾ cup vegetable oil
- 10 to 15 curry leaves (optional)
- 1 cup peeled and chopped tomatoes
- 5 teaspoons sugar
- Kosher salt

1 In a small bowl, soak the dried shrimp in ¼ cup vinegar for at least 4 hours. Strain and squeeze the vinegar from the shrimp into another bowl. Mince the shrimp finely by hand or in a food processor.

2 In a spice grinder or mortar and pestle, grind the chiles, ginger, garlic, and 2 tablespoons of vinegar until finely chopped and the seeds of the chiles are not visible. If the paste is too dry, loosen it with some shrimp-infused vinegar.

3 Heat the oil in a medium saucepan over medium heat until it's shimmering. Add the curry leaves (if using) and cook until fragrant. Turn the heat to low. Add the ground chile mixture and tomatoes and cook, stirring frequently, until the oil floats to the top of the masala paste. Be careful to stand back, as it tends to bubble and spurt.

4 Add the minced shrimp, sugar, and remaining ¾ cup vinegar, and cook on low for about 20 minutes, stirring occasionally. Season with salt. The finished pickles should be tangy, sweet, hot, and salty.

5 Transfer the mixture to a glass jar with a lid and let it cool to room temperature. Screw on the lid and store the pickles in the refrigerator. Allow the pickles to mature for 2 to 4 weeks before serving. The pickles can be stored in the refrigerator for up to 1 year.

Serving Tip: Pickles are eaten in small quantities of a tablespoon or less at a time. Pickles must be served with a separate dry, clean spoon, because they spoil easily when cross-contaminated with other spoons at the table.

NO-OIL, NO-COOK LIME PICKLES

Nimmakaya Uragaya

SOUTH INDIA

VEGAN
GLUTEN-FREE
PEANUT-FREE
SOY-FREE
ALLIUM-FREE

MAKES ABOUT 1 POUND ♦ PREP TIME: 30 MINUTES PLUS 1 HOUR TO DRY AND 4 DAYS TO SIT ♦ PICKLING TIME: 2 TO 3 WEEKS ♦ SHELF LIFE: 2 MONTHS

There are hundreds of pickle recipes in India, and most of them use oil as a preservative. In this recipe from Andhra Pradesh, however, limes and rock salt are used instead. Feel free to reduce the amount of chili powder to suit your taste, but don't leave it out, as its flavor is needed to balance the bitterness of the lime.

6 to 8 Indian or key limes
½ cup powdered rock salt
1 tablespoon turmeric powder
¼ cup red chili powder
1 teaspoon asafetida
½ teaspoon fenugreek seeds, dry roasted and ground to a powder

1 Wash and dry the limes thoroughly. Wipe each with a clean, dry cloth and leave them in the sun for about an hour. Set half of the limes aside and cut the remaining limes into 4 wedges each, removing as many seeds as possible. Pack the cut limes into a glass or ceramic jar with a lid.

2 Cut the remaining limes in half and squeeze their juices into a bowl. Stir in the rock salt and turmeric. Pour this juice over the limes in the jar.

3 Screw on the lid and shake the jar vigorously. Store the jar in a dry location at room temperature for 4 days, stirring once a day with a clean, dry spoon.

4 On the fifth day, stir the chili powder, asafetida, and fenugreek into the pickles. Cover and shake the jar to mix well.

5 Allow the pickles to mature for 2 to 3 weeks before serving. Serve with an Indian meal or Indian snacks like Easy Rice and Lentil Crêpes (page 97) or Amritsari Flatbread (page 94).

Substitution Tip: If you can't find powdered rock salt, use regular kosher salt instead, but reduce the quantity of salt by one-quarter.

Ingredient Tip: If the limes are still too bitter for your taste after the pickling time in this recipe, let them mature for more days or weeks until they're to your liking.

6

VEGETARIAN AND DALS

SAVORY GRATED FRESH CORN

Bhutte ka Kees

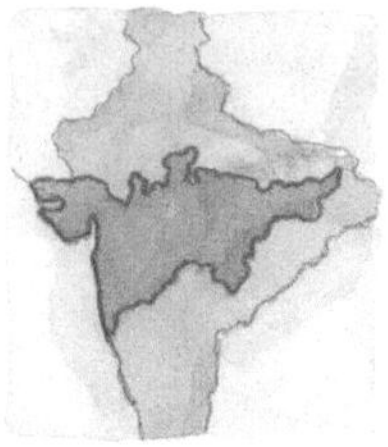

WEST AND CENTRAL INDIA

VEGETARIAN
EGG-FREE
GLUTEN-FREE
PEANUT-FREE
SOY-FREE
ALLIUM-FREE

SERVES 2 ◆ PREP TIME: 10 MINUTES ◆ COOK TIME: 12 MINUTES *In the central Indian state of Madhya Pradesh, bhutte ka kees is made when corn is in season and is served as a breakfast or snack dish on every street corner. The sweetness of the corn is beautifully balanced by the minimal spices. To make this dish vegan, you can use water or coconut milk instead of milk.*

3 medium ears of corn
2 teaspoons vegetable oil
1 teaspoon black mustard seeds
Pinch asafetida
2 green chiles, seeded and chopped
8 curry leaves (optional)
½ teaspoon turmeric powder
½ teaspoon red chili powder
Kosher salt
½ cup milk
2 tablespoons freshly squeezed lime juice
2 tablespoons finely chopped cilantro leaves
2 to 3 lime wedges

1 Using a box grater, finely grate the corn, removing all the kernels from the cobs.

2 In a medium skillet or kadhai, heat the oil over medium heat until it's shimmering. Add the mustard seeds and wait for them to pop. Quickly add the asafetida and stir. Add the chiles and curry leaves (if using), and stir until aromatic, about 20 seconds.

3 Add the corn, turmeric, and chili powder, and stir. Season with salt.

4 Reduce the heat to low, add the milk, cover, and cook until the corn is tender, about 10 minutes, stirring once in the process. Add the lime juice and mix well. Turn off the heat and transfer to a serving dish.

5 Serve warm, garnished with cilantro leaves and lime wedges on the side.

Substitution Tip: If you can't get fresh corn, you can use frozen kernels instead. Thaw them completely, then pulse them in the food processor just until coarsely chopped.

POTATO AND TOMATO CURRY

Aloo Tamatar ka Jhol

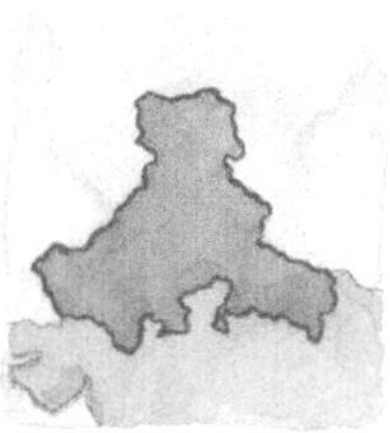

NORTH INDIA

VEGETARIAN
EGG-FREE
GLUTEN-FREE
PEANUT-FREE
SOY-FREE

SERVES 4 ◆ PREP TIME: 20 MINUTES ◆ COOK TIME: 20 MINUTES Jhol *is the name for a curry or gravy that is a little on the thin side. This simple potato and tomato curry from Uttarakhand is delicious with rice or bread, and is particularly comforting when the weather is a little nippy.*

- 2 tablespoons ghee
- 1 teaspoon cumin seeds
- ¼ teaspoon fenugreek seeds
- 1 tablespoon finely chopped garlic
- 1½ teaspoons finely chopped ginger
- ½ cup chopped red onion
- 1 teaspoon red chili powder
- ½ teaspoon turmeric powder
- 3 large tomatoes, chopped
- 2 cups potatoes, peeled and cubed
- Kosher salt
- 1 cup water
- ½ teaspoon Punjabi Garam Masala (page 45)
- 1 tablespoon cilantro leaves

1 Melt the ghee in a medium saucepan or kadhai over medium heat until it begins to shimmer. Add the cumin and fenugreek seeds and wait until they splutter.

2 Add the garlic and ginger and stir until aromatic, 20 to 30 seconds. Add the onion and sauté until it's tender and light brown. Add the chili powder and turmeric and stir until the powders stain the oil, about 10 seconds.

3 Add the tomatoes and sauté for about 5 minutes until they soften. You can help this along by mashing the tomatoes with the back of the spoon. Add the potatoes and salt, stirring well, then add the water. Bring to a boil and reduce the heat to low; simmer for 10 to 15 minutes, or until the potatoes are cooked through and a bit crumbly. continued ▶

4 In the last 5 minutes of cooking, sprinkle on the garam masala and allow it to cook for 5 minutes. Serve hot, garnished with the cilantro leaves. Serve with rice, Millet Pilaf (page 88), or Amritsari Flatbread (page 94).

Make It Faster: You can make this dish even faster by using preboiled potatoes. Boil the potatoes in salted water in an electric pressure cooker at high pressure for 4 minutes. Use the quick method to release the pressure. Reduce the cooking time at step 3 by half.

Substitution Tip: An easy way to make this vegan is to use vegetable oil instead of ghee.

ALOO GOBI

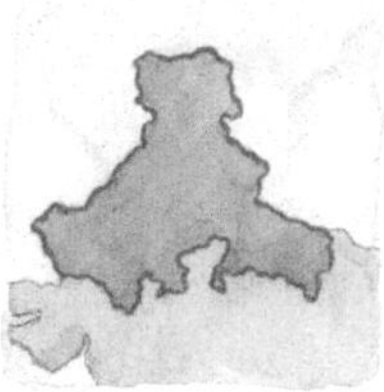

NORTH INDIA

VEGAN
GLUTEN-FREE
PEANUT-FREE
SOY-FREE
ALLIUM-FREE

SERVES 2 ♦ PREP TIME: 20 MINUTES ♦ COOK TIME: 20 MINUTES *I find this classic vegetarian dish from Himachal Pradesh very comforting. It's easy to make and asks for only the freshest ingredients. The recipe here is for a dry version of the dish, which can be scooped up with Plain Naan (page 92) or enjoyed with a meal of Plain Basmati Rice (page 76) and dal.*

- 2 tablespoons vegetable oil
- 1 teaspoon cumin seeds
- Pinch asafetida
- 1 green chile, finely chopped
- 2 teaspoons minced fresh ginger
- 1 garlic clove, minced
- 1 cup peeled and roughly chopped potatoes
- 1½ cups medium cauliflower florets
- Kosher salt
- 2 tablespoons water
- ½ teaspoon turmeric powder
- 1 teaspoon red chili powder
- ½ teaspoon Punjabi Garam Masala (page 45)
- 1 teaspoon dried raw mango powder (amchur)
- 1 tablespoon chopped cilantro leaves

1 Heat the oil in a medium saucepan over medium heat until it is shimmering. Add the cumin seeds and let them splutter. Add the asafetida and stir, about 10 seconds. Turn the heat to low, add the chile, ginger, and garlic, and cook until the mixture is aromatic, about 30 seconds. Add the potatoes and stir. Cover and cook about 5 to 7 minutes, until the potatoes soften, stirring occasionally if they tend to stick.

2 Add the cauliflower, salt, and water. Stir and cover. Increase the heat to medium and cook for 7 to 8 minutes, stirring occasionally.

3 Add the turmeric, chili powder, garam masala, and mango powder. Add a little water if the cauliflower and potato are still not soft. Cover and cook, stirring occasionally, until everything is tender and the water has cooked away. Garnish with cilantro leaves and serve with Plain Naan (page 92).

Cooking Tip: Add water a little at a time and stir the cauliflower carefully, or the florets will break up and become messy.

VEGETABLE MAKHANWALA

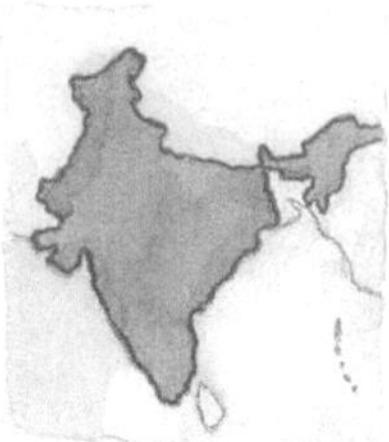

ALL INDIA

VEGETARIAN
EGG-FREE
GLUTEN-FREE
PEANUT-FREE
SOY-FREE

SERVES 2 TO 3 ◆ PREP TIME: 20 MINUTES, PLUS 15 MINUTES TO SOAK ◆ COOK TIME: 20 MINUTES Vegetable makhanwala *means "vegetables cooked in a rich, buttery gravy." Ghee and cashew paste are integral to giving the dish its creaminess. You can add any assortment of vegetables to the dish; just remember to cut them into pieces of the same size so they cook evenly. I like to eat this with a side of Mango Pickles (page 118) and some Plain Naan (page 92).*

10 cashews
½ cup water
1 tablespoon vegetable oil
1 tablespoon unsalted butter or ghee, plus 1 teaspoon for garnish
2 green chiles, finely chopped
1 tablespoon Ginger-Garlic Paste (page 46)
2 green cardamom pods
½ cup tomato purée or 2 fresh tomatoes, run through a blender
1 tablespoon ground coriander
1 teaspoon red chili powder
1 teaspoon turmeric powder
¼ cup chopped carrot
¼ cup chopped potato
¼ cup fresh, or frozen and thawed, peas
¼ cup chopped fresh, or frozen and thawed, green beans
¼ cup chopped cauliflower florets
1 tablespoon water
1 teaspoon Punjabi Garam Masala (page 45)
1 tablespoon dried fenugreek leaves (optional)
Kosher salt

1 In a small bowl, soak the cashews in ½ cup water for about 15 minutes to soften. Strain the nuts, reserving the water. Transfer the cashews to a blender or spice grinder with a couple of tablespoons of the reserved water and process them until they form a fine paste. Set aside.

2 In a large, heavy saucepan or kadhai, heat the oil and 1 tablespoon of butter together over medium heat. When the butter is melted and the mixture begins to shimmer, add the chiles, ginger-garlic paste, and cardamom and sauté until fragrant, about 30 seconds.

3 Add the tomato purée and cook until it reduces a bit and the oil floats up to the top, stirring constantly. (If you're using blended fresh tomatoes, this might take a bit longer, as the water content will be greater. For fresh tomatoes, cover the saucepan, turn the heat to medium-low, and allow the tomatoes to reduce for about 10 minutes, stirring occasionally.)

4 Add the coriander, chili powder, and turmeric, mix well, and cook for 2 more minutes. The oil should separate even more. Add the cashew paste to the pan and mix well until it is fully incorporated. Cook for 5 to 7 minutes, stirring occasionally, as cashew paste tends to stick to the bottom of the pan.

5 Add the carrot, potato, peas, green beans, cauliflower, water, garam masala, and dried fenugreek leaves (if using). Cover the pan and let the curry cook over low heat for about 10 minutes, allowing the spices to blend. Taste the curry and season with salt. Garnish with a little melted ghee or butter and serve hot with Indian breads like Plain Naan (page 92) or Amritsari Flatbread (page 94), or with Plain Basmati Rice (page 76).

Make It Healthier: You can add a tablespoon of plain yogurt instead of butter to garnish the dish.

SPICED, STUFFED EGGPLANT

Baingan ki Lonje

NORTH INDIA

VEGETARIAN
EGG-FREE
GLUTEN-FREE
PEANUT-FREE
SOY-FREE

SERVES 4 ◆ PREP TIME: 15 MINUTES ◆ COOK TIME: 15 MINUTES *The humble eggplant has countless preparations in India. This stuffed version uses simple spices to lift the mild flavor of the vegetable. It is rather spicy because of the chiles and ground spices, but you can moderate these to suit your taste. Make it vegan by substituting vegetable oil for the ghee.*

FOR THE MASALA PASTE

- 2 tablespoons ghee, divided
- 1 cup sliced red onion
- 1 teaspoon chopped fresh ginger
- Kosher salt
- 2 teaspoons sugar
- 2 whole red Kashmiri chiles or green chiles
- 5 whole cloves, divided
- 1 (1-inch) cinnamon stick
- Seeds from 1 small black cardamom pod
- ½ teaspoon peppercorns

FOR THE EGGPLANT

- 8 long, thin, dark Asian eggplants, halved lengthwise, though the stalks
- 1 tablespoon freshly squeezed lemon juice
- 1 tablespoon chopped cilantro leaves

To make the masala paste

1 Melt 1 tablespoon of the ghee in a frying pan over medium heat until it begins to shimmer. Add the onion and sauté until brown and crisp, stirring frequently. Transfer the onion to a small bowl to cool. Turn off the heat and return the pan to the stove.

2 Using a mortar and pestle or spice grinder, grind the onion, ginger, salt, sugar, chiles, 2 cloves, cinnamon, cardamom seeds, and peppercorns until you have a smooth paste.

To make the eggplant

1 Using a spoon, apply a thick layer of this paste to the cut side of each eggplant to stuff it.

2 In the same frying pan, melt the remaining tablespoon of ghee until it shimmers. Add the remaining 3 cloves and stir until they are aromatic, about 10 seconds. Reduce the heat to low and add the eggplants to the pan, cut-sides up. Flip carefully 1 or 2 times until they are cooked through, about 12 minutes, depending on the thickness of the eggplants.

3 During the last minute of cooking, drizzle with lemon juice. Remove from the pan and garnish with cilantro leaves.

Serving Tip: Enjoy this with Indian flatbreads like Amritsari Flatbread (page 94) or with a dal like Tangy Whole Red Lentils (page 150).

STUFFED BELL PEPPERS

Bharwaan Shimla Mirch

NORTH INDIA

VEGAN
GLUTEN-FREE
PEANUT-FREE
SOY-FREE

SERVES 4 ♦ PREP TIME: 20 MINUTES ♦ COOK TIME: 35 MINUTES

Stuffed vegetables are quite popular among Indians who follow a vegetarian diet. This stuffed bell pepper dish uses potato as the main stuffing ingredient, along with peas and some spices. The peppers aren't spicy at all and lend a really nice texture to the dish. Choose peppers with a steady base so they can stand up in the pan.

- 4 large green bell peppers
- 3 tablespoons vegetable oil, divided
- ½ teaspoon cumin seeds
- 1 small red onion, finely chopped
- 1 green chile, chopped
- ½ teaspoon dried raw mango powder (amchur) or 1 teaspoon freshly squeezed lime juice
- ¼ teaspoon turmeric powder
- ½ teaspoon red chili powder
- 7 ounces boiled and mashed potatoes
- ½ cup green peas, blanched
- ½ teaspoon Punjabi Garam Masala (page 45) or Basic Homemade Garam Masala (page 44)
- Kosher salt
- 1 tablespoon chopped cilantro leaves

1 Slice off the tops of the bell peppers and set them aside. Using a clean kitchen towel, wipe the surface of the peppers to ensure that they are dry. Remove and discard the seeds and white membranes from the insides of the peppers.

2 Preheat the oven to 400°F.

3 In a medium skillet, heat 1½ tablespoons of oil over medium heat. Add the cumin seeds. When they crackle, add the onion and sauté until softened. Stir in the chile, mango powder, turmeric, and chili powder.

4 Add the mashed potatoes, peas, and garam masala. Mix well. Season with salt. Continue cooking for 1 minute. Turn off the heat and allow the mixture to cool.

5 Stuff the bell peppers with this mixture and cover them with their tops. Set the peppers upright in a baking pan that will hold them snugly. Brush with the remaining 1½ tablespoons of oil and place them in the oven.

6 Cook for 20 to 30 minutes, until the peppers are tender and browned in spots. Top with the chopped cilantro and serve with warm Indian bread, or as a side dish.

Make It Easier: The peppers can also be cooked in a saucepan. Heat 1½ tablespoons oil over medium heat in the saucepan until it's shimmering. Turn the heat to low and place the stuffed bell peppers in the pan, sitting upright. Cook uncovered on low, and at intervals turn the bell peppers on their sides; keep turning until all sides are well cooked. It takes 25 to 30 minutes on low until the skins get wrinkled and golden brown.

STIR-FRIED GREEN BEANS AND COCONUT

Green Beans Foogath

ALL INDIA

VEGAN
GLUTEN-FREE
PEANUT-FREE
SOY-FREE

SERVES 2 ♦ PREP TIME: 10 MINUTES ♦ COOK TIME: 10 TO 15 MINUTES

In Goan cuisine, foogath *is the term used for any vegetable stir-fry with coconut. The beauty of this style of cooking is that the veggies retain their crunch and you get the actual flavor of the vegetable in the dish, since it is so mildly spiced. This is the perfect dish to add balance to a spice-heavy main course.*

9 ounces green beans
1 tablespoon coconut or vegetable oil
1 teaspoon black mustard seeds
1 medium red onion, finely chopped
10 curry leaves (optional)
2 green or red chiles, split in half lengthwise
Pinch sugar
Kosher salt
½ cup fresh, or frozen and thawed, grated coconut

1 Wash, trim, and chop the beans into ½-inch or smaller pieces. Set aside.

2 In a saucepan, heat the oil over medium heat until it's shimmering. Add the mustard seeds and let them crackle. Add the onion and sauté until it's softened. If it begins to brown, add a little water to the pan.

3 Add the curry leaves (if using), and stir until they become aromatic, about 10 seconds. Add the chiles and stir for an additional 20 seconds. Add the beans and sugar. Season with salt.

4 Cover the saucepan with a lid. Heat about ½ cup of water until it's hot, and have it on hand for adding to the beans as needed. Check the beans every 2 to 3 minutes, stirring carefully from the bottom of the pan. If the beans begin to stick, add a few drops of water at a time to aid in cooking.

5 When the beans are nearly done but still crunchy, add the coconut and stir well. Continue cooking for 2 to 5 more minutes. Serve hot with Indian bread or rice and dal.

Substitution Tip: Traditionally, cabbage or green beans are used in a foogath, but you can add cauliflower, fava beans, or any combination of vegetables you like.

VEGETABLES COOKED IN YOGURT SAUCE

Mor Kuzhambu

SOUTH INDIA

VEGETARIAN
EGG-FREE
GLUTEN-FREE
PEANUT-FREE
SOY-FREE
ALLIUM-FREE

SERVES 2 ♦ PREP TIME: 15 MINUTES ♦ COOK TIME: 20 MINUTES *This is a simple dish from Tamil Nadu that is very versatile. You can add any vegetable of your choice, and it's ready in a matter of minutes.* Kuzhambu *in the Tamil language refers to a broth, gravy, or sauce that is made with lentils and tamarind. The word* mor *refers to the kuzhambu being made with yogurt instead of lentils.*

- ½ cup fresh, or frozen and thawed, grated coconut
- 2 teaspoons coriander seeds
- 1 (½-inch) piece fresh ginger
- 3 teaspoons cumin seeds
- 2 green chiles
- 3 teaspoons vegetable or coconut oil, divided
- 18 curry leaves (optional), divided
- 1 cup plain yogurt, whisked smooth
- 1 teaspoon turmeric powder
- Kosher salt
- ¾ cup chopped fresh vegetables of your choice (cauliflower, carrots, green beans, etc.)
- 1 teaspoon black mustard seeds
- 1 dried red chile, broken in two

1 In a spice grinder or mortar and pestle, process the coconut, coriander seeds, ginger, cumin seeds, and chiles until they form a thick, smooth paste. If needed, add a little water to aid in the grinding. Set aside.

2 In a small saucepan, heat 1½ teaspoons of oil over medium heat until it begins to shimmer. Add 10 of the curry leaves (if using), and allow them to crackle, about 20 seconds. Then add the ground coconut-chile mixture to the oil and cook, stirring constantly, for 1 minute. Remove the pan from the heat. Transfer the spice mixture to a medium bowl and whisk in the yogurt. Add the turmeric and season with salt. Stir in the vegetables.

3 Transfer the vegetable mixture to a medium saucepan and cook the vegetables over low heat, uncovered, for about 15 minutes, or until tender. Do not bring the mixture to a boil. When the vegetables are fork tender, transfer them to a serving bowl. *continued* ▶

4 In a small skillet, heat the remaining 1½ teaspoons of oil over medium heat until it begins to shimmer. Add the mustard seeds and wait until they begin to crackle, 10 to 15 seconds. Add the dried chile and cook, stirring frequently, until it begins to darken in color, about 10 seconds.

5 Add the remaining 8 curry leaves (if using), swirl them in the oil, and cook for another 30 seconds until fragrant. Immediately remove the skillet from the heat and pour this oil over the vegetables, leaving the solids in the skillet. Serve the vegetables and sauce with Plain Basmati Rice (page 76).

Cooking Tip: To keep the yogurt from curdling, make sure you whisk it really well in step 2, and do not cover the dish while cooking or allow it to boil.

VEGETABLE AND NOODLE SOUP

Thenthuk

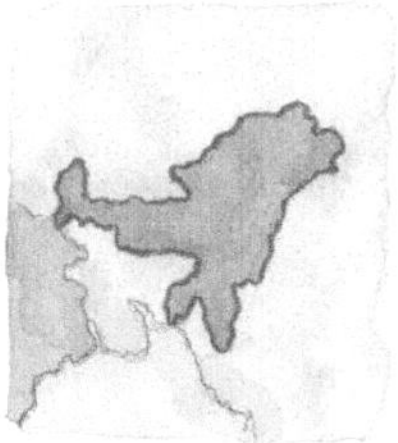

NORTHEAST INDIA

VEGAN
PEANUT-FREE

SERVES 2 ◆ PREP TIME: 15 MINUTES ◆ COOK TIME: 20 MINUTES *Similar to Tibetan thukpa, thenthuk is a pulled noodle soup from Arunachal Pradesh. The noodles are traditionally made at home and then flattened by hand and blanched in the broth. In my recipe, though, I have used ready-made noodles to save on time, and the broth is just as delicious.*

- 2 teaspoons vegetable oil
- 2 tablespoons chopped red onion
- 1 teaspoon Ginger-Garlic Paste (page 46)
- 1 medium tomato, chopped
- Kosher salt
- 1½ cups vegetable stock
- 1 teaspoon soy sauce
- 1 medium potato, chopped
- 1 tablespoon chopped radish
- ½ cup wheat noodles
- ½ cup spinach, chopped
- 2 tablespoons chopped cilantro leaves

1 In a saucepan, wok, or kadhai, heat the oil over medium heat until it's shimmering. Add the chopped onion and garlic-ginger paste, and sauté until the onion is soft and the paste is fragrant. Add the chopped tomatoes and cook until they begin breaking apart. Season with salt.

2 Add the vegetable stock, soy sauce, potato, and radish, and cook until tender. Add the noodles into the boiling stock and cook until they are done, about 10 minutes. Add the spinach and cilantro at the last minute of cooking, or even when the broth is off the heat, just to blanch. Stir and serve warm as a soup.

Substitution Tip: For the gluten-intolerant, use rice noodles.

HOMEMADE PANEER

ALL INDIA

VEGETARIAN
EGG-FREE
GLUTEN-FREE
PEANUT-FREE
SOY-FREE
ALLIUM-FREE

SERVES 2 ◆ PREP TIME: 10 MINUTES, PLUS 30 MINUTES TO REST ◆ COOK TIME: 15 MINUTES *Many vegetarian Indians use paneer as a source of protein in their diet. It's really easy to make, with just two ingredients, and keeps well for about two days. Once you've learned the art of making paneer at home, you can experiment with it in various curries, and as an addition to many vegetarian dishes in this book.*

1 quart full-fat milk

2 teaspoons freshly squeezed lemon juice, white vinegar, or plain yogurt

1 Bring the milk to a boil in a saucepan. Add the lemon juice, vinegar, or yogurt and stir through. The milk will curdle.

2 Pour this curdled milk through a piece of cheesecloth draped over a colander to strain it. Bundle the cheesecloth tightly around the strained milk solids and squeeze out as much liquid as possible.

3 Place this cheesecloth bundle on a plate and put a weight on it, such as a pot with a brick inside, to remove any remaining water and shape it into a firm cheese. Allow it to sit for at least 30 minutes.

4 Remove the cheese from the cheesecloth and cut into cubes. Your homemade paneer is ready. Refrigerate in an airtight container for up to 2 days.

Serving Tip: You can have freshly made paneer as is, with a sprinkling of kosher salt and Roasted Cumin Powder (page 42).

PALAK PANEER

NORTH INDIA

VEGETARIAN
EGG-FREE
GLUTEN-FREE
PEANUT-FREE
SOY-FREE

SERVES 2 ◆ PREP TIME: 20 MINUTES ◆ COOK TIME: 30 MINUTES

The combination of puréed, silky spinach (palak) and fragrant spices, mingled with the richness of paneer, makes this dish a delight. It's quite popular in the north of India, where milk products are a staple, and the addition of spinach gives it a fresh green color that contrasts with the usual yellows and reds of Indian curries.

FOR THE SPINACH

1 teaspoon vegetable oil
½ teaspoon cumin seeds
1 teaspoon Ginger-Garlic Paste (page 46)
Seeds from 1 cardamom pod
1 green chile, split lengthwise, stem discarded
4 cups chopped spinach

FOR THE CURRY

2 tablespoons oil
1 Indian bay leaf or Mediterranean bay leaf
½ cup finely chopped red onion
½ cup finely chopped tomato
1 teaspoon Ginger-Garlic Paste (page 46)
1 teaspoon red chili powder
1 teaspoon Roasted Cumin Powder (page 42)
1 teaspoon Punjabi Garam Masala (page 45)
Pinch sugar
Kosher salt
1½ cups cubed paneer
1 tablespoon heavy cream

To make the spinach

1 Heat the oil in a large saucepan over medium heat until it begins to shimmer. Add the cumin seeds and let them splutter for a few seconds. Add the ginger-garlic paste and cook, stirring constantly, for about 20 seconds. Add the cardamom seeds and chile and stir until fragrant, about 10 seconds. *continued* ▶

2 Add the spinach and stir to combine. It may seem like a lot of spinach, but it will wilt considerably. Cook uncovered for about 5 minutes, stirring occasionally. Resist the urge to add water to the pan at this point, as the spinach will release its own liquid as it cooks. Do not let the spinach cook for longer than 5 minutes, though, because if it cooks too long, it will lose its bright-green color.

3 Take the saucepan off the heat and allow the spinach to cool. Then process it to a fine purée in a blender.

To make the curry

1 Heat the oil in a clean, medium saucepan over medium heat until it begins to shimmer. Add the bay leaf and onion and cook until the onion is softened, about 7 minutes. If the onion browns too quickly, add a few drops of water and stir. Add the tomato and cook until softened, 2 to 3 minutes. Add the ginger-garlic paste and stir for about 10 seconds, then stir in the chili powder and cumin powder.

2 Add the spinach purée to the pan and cook for about 5 minutes, stirring constantly. Add the garam masala and sugar, and season with salt. Stir in the cubed paneer and let the mixture cook for 5 minutes.

3 Transfer the Palak Paneer to a serving bowl, garnish with cream, and serve with Plain Naan (page 92) or as a side to any Indian main dish.

Cooking Tip: To retain the vibrant green of the spinach, blanch the spinach, plunge it in ice water, and then purée it with the spices.

PANEER IN RED GRAVY

Wozij Chaaman

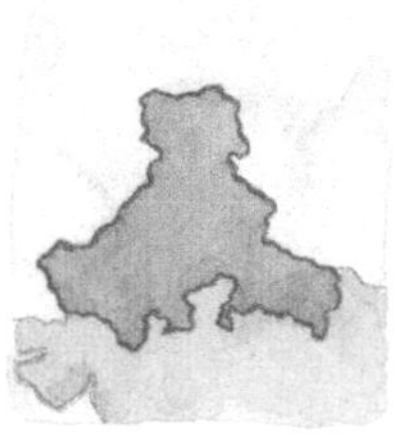

NORTH INDIA

VEGETARIAN
EGG-FREE
GLUTEN-FREE
PEANUT-FREE
SOY-FREE
ALLIUM-FREE

SERVES 2 ♦ PREP TIME: 10 MINUTES ♦ COOK TIME: 15 TO 20 MINUTES *The color of this dish has to be seen to be believed. Kashmiri red chili powder gives a scarlet hue to the finished dish, which tastes as appetizing as it looks. This is an important dish in Kashmiri cuisine and one that is prepared for special occasions. Full of warming spices, it's perfect on a cold winter day.*

- 2 to 3 tablespoons vegetable oil
- 10 ounces paneer, cut into cubes
- 2 teaspoons ground fennel seeds
- ½ teaspoon grated fresh ginger
- 1 Indian bay leaf or Mediterranean bay leaf
- 2 (1-inch) cinnamon sticks
- ¾ cup water, divided
- Kosher salt
- 1 teaspoon cumin seeds
- 2 whole cloves
- Pinch asafetida
- ¾ tablespoon Kashmiri red chili powder
- 1 black cardamom pod
- 3 green cardamom pods
- 1 teaspoon black cumin seeds

1 In a small saucepan, heat the oil over medium heat until it's shimmering. Add the paneer and sauté until golden brown, 5 to 7 minutes. Using a slotted spoon, transfer the paneer to another saucepan. Keep the oil warm over low heat.

2 Place the saucepan with the paneer on the stove top, but don't turn on the heat yet. Add the fennel, ginger, bay leaf, cinnamon, and ½ cup water to the pan, and season with salt.

3 Increase the heat under the other saucepan, with the oil, to medium and add the cumin seeds, allowing them to sizzle briefly. Stir in the cloves and asafetida. Add the chili powder and stir briskly for 10 to 15 seconds, until the oil turns red, taking care not to burn it. Immediately add the remaining ¼ cup water and cook out the water for 2 to 3 minutes, until the mixture is fairly dry.

4 Pour the red oil mixture into the saucepan with the paneer. Turn the heat to low and add the black and green cardamom pods and black cumin. Cook until half the water evaporates. Serve hot with white rice.

PANEER CURRY WITH BUTTER

Paneer Makhani

WEST AND CENTRAL INDIA

VEGETARIAN
EGG-FREE
GLUTEN-FREE
PEANUT-FREE
SOY-FREE
ALLIUM-FREE

SERVES 4 ◆ PREP TIME: 15 MINUTES ◆ COOK TIME: 20 MINUTES *Paneer finds its way into many recipes across the country and is a great source of protein for India's many vegetarians. Though* paneer makhani *literally means "cottage cheese in a buttery gravy," this recipe from Gujarat uses cashew paste to mimic the creaminess of a cream-based sauce and give you a dish that is every bit as flavorful and even more hearty.*

10 cashews
½ cup water
1 tablespoon vegetable oil
1 tablespoon unsalted butter or ghee, plus 1 teaspoon for garnish
2 green chiles, finely chopped
1 (1-inch) piece fresh ginger, slivered
2 green cardamom pods
1 cup tomato purée or 4 fresh tomatoes, blended
1 tablespoon ground coriander
3 teaspoons red chili powder
1 teaspoon turmeric powder
9 ounces paneer, cut into 1-inch cubes
1 tablespoon milk or water
1 teaspoon Basic Homemade Garam Masala (page 44)
1 tablespoon dried fenugreek leaves (optional)
Kosher salt

1 In a small bowl, soak the cashews in ½ cup of water for about 15 minutes. Strain the nuts, reserving the water. Transfer the cashews to a blender or spice grinder with 2 tablespoons of the reserved water, and blend to a fine paste. Add another tablespoon of reserved water if the paste seems too dry.

2 In a heavy saucepan or kadhai, heat the oil and 1 tablespoon of butter together on medium heat. When the butter has melted and the mixture begins to shimmer, add the chiles, ginger, and cardamom and sauté until fragrant, about 30 seconds.

3 Add the tomato purée and cook until it reduces a bit and the oil floats to the top of the mixture, stirring constantly. (If you're using blended fresh tomatoes, this might take a bit longer, as the water content will be greater. For fresh tomatoes, cover the saucepan and turn the heat to medium-low and allow the tomatoes to reduce for about 10 minutes, stirring occasionally.)

4 Add the coriander, chili powder, and turmeric, mix well, and cook for 2 more minutes. The oil should separate even more. Add the cashew paste and mix well. Cook for 5 to 7 minutes, stirring occasionally, as cashew paste tends to stick to the bottom of the pan.

5 Stir in the paneer cubes, milk or water, garam masala, and dried fenugreek leaves (if using). Cover and let the curry cook on low for 5 to 7 minutes, allowing the spices to blend. Season with salt. Garnish with the remaining butter and serve hot with Indian breads, or with Plain Basmati Rice (page 76).

Ingredient Tip: If you are using frozen paneer, keep the paneer on the countertop for 10 to 15 minutes before cooking.

CREAMY LENTILS

Dal Makhani

NORTH INDIA

VEGETARIAN
EGG-FREE
GLUTEN-FREE
PEANUT-FREE
SOY-FREE

SERVES 2 ◆ PREP TIME: 15 MINUTES, PLUS OVERNIGHT TO SOAK ◆ COOK TIME: 1½ TO 2 HOURS *The Punjabis' love affair with dal makhani is legendary. Traditionally, this creamy, rich lentil dish is cooked over a very low flame through the night and into the morning, then embellished with spices and cream and left to simmer a little while longer. In this home-style recipe, you can re-create the same creaminess either by pressure cooking or by slow cooking.*

- ⅓ cup whole black lentils (urad dal)
- 2 tablespoons kidney beans
- 2 cups plus 2 tablespoons water, divided
- 1 tablespoon butter
- 1½ teaspoons vegetable oil
- ½ teaspoon cumin seeds
- 1 (1-inch) cinnamon stick
- 2 whole cloves
- 2 green cardamom pods
- 1 green chile, split in half lengthwise
- 1 medium red onion, finely chopped
- 2 teaspoons Ginger-Garlic Paste (page 46)
- 1 teaspoon red chili powder
- ½ teaspoon turmeric powder
- 2 tablespoons tomato purée
- Kosher salt
- 1 tablespoon chopped cilantro leaves
- 1½ teaspoons fresh cream

1 Soak the lentils and kidney beans overnight. Drain.

2 In a large pot, mix the lentils and beans with 2 cups of water. Bring to a boil, then reduce the heat to low and simmer, covered, for 1 to 1½ hours, until all the beans are softened. Stir occasionally, and add more water, ½ cup at a time, if the dal is drying up while cooking. When the dal is finished cooking, use a large spoon to slightly mash the beans and lentils in the pot.

3 Heat the butter and oil in a large saucepan over medium heat until the butter melts and the mixture shimmers. Add the cumin seeds. When they crackle, stir in the cinnamon, cloves, cardamom, and chile. Add the onion and sauté until golden brown, then stir in the ginger-garlic paste, chili powder, turmeric, and tomato purée. Turn off the heat and let the mixture cool until the oil separates from the spices.

4 Add the dal to the saucepan and season with salt. Add about 2 tablespoons water, then adjust the seasonings as desired. Cook for 10 to 15 minutes over medium heat, until the flavors are blended.

5 Serve hot, garnished with the cilantro and cream.

Make It Faster: Cook the soaked dal for about 25 minutes in the electric pressure cooker on high pressure. Use the quick method to release the pressure. Transfer to a saucepan and resume following the recipe, starting with step 3.

Make It Easier: Place the soaked dal in the slow cooker on Low for 7 to 8 hours. Open the lid and follow step 3 right in the slow cooker. Resume following the recipe, starting with step 4.

SWEET AND SOUR LENTILS

Khatti Meethi Dal

WEST AND CENTRAL INDIA

VEGAN
GLUTEN-FREE
PEANUT-FREE
SOY-FREE
ALLIUM-FREE

SERVES 4 ♦ PREP TIME: 15 MINUTES ♦ COOK TIME: 1 HOUR, 15 MINUTES

This is a classic meal from Gujarat. It's packed with protein and fiber, and the mild spiciness of the broth is perfect for those who are new to the world of Indian dals. It tastes wonderful with plain and simple white rice, which is the way I like to have it.

- 3½ tablespoons vegetable oil, divided
- ½ cup split pigeon peas (tuvar dal)
- 2 tablespoons small cubed radish
- ½ teaspoon turmeric powder
- 2½ cups water, divided
- Kosher salt
- 2 tablespoons fresh, or frozen and thawed, grated coconut
- ½ teaspoon black mustard seeds
- 1 teaspoon cumin seeds
- 8 curry leaves (optional)
- ¼ teaspoon asafetida
- 1 tablespoon tamarind pulp
- 1 tablespoon grated jaggery
- 1 teaspoon red chili powder
- 2 teaspoons ground coriander
- 1 tablespoon chopped cilantro leaves

1 Heat 2 tablespoons oil in a medium saucepan over medium heat until it's shimmering. Add the pigeon peas, radishes, turmeric, and 2 cups of water. Season with salt. Cook over medium-low heat, covered, until the dal is tender, about 1 hour. Remove the pan from the heat and let the dal cool, then mash it a bit with a large spoon. Set aside.

2 In a dry skillet over medium heat, roast the coconut until it is lightly browned. Cool, then grind it finely in a spice grinder or mortar and pestle.

3 Heat 1½ tablespoons of oil in a medium saucepan over medium heat until it's shimmering. Add the mustard and cumin seeds and stir until they crackle. Add the curry leaves (if using) and asafetida, stirring for about 10 seconds until aromatic.

4 Add the cooked dal, coconut powder, tamarind pulp, jaggery, chili powder, ground coriander, and the remaining ½ cup water to the pan. Bring to a boil, reduce the heat to low, and simmer for 5 to 7 minutes. Serve hot, garnished with cilantro leaves.

Make It Faster: Cook the dal with kosher salt and turmeric in an electric pressure cooker for 15 to 18 minutes at high pressure. Use the quick method to release the pressure. Open the lid, and when cool, mash the dal a bit with a large spoon. Follow steps 2 through 4 as written.

Make It Easier: Cook the dal with kosher salt and turmeric in a slow cooker for 3 hours on High or 6 to 8 hours on Low. Open the lid, and when cool, mash the dal a bit with a large spoon. Follow steps 2 through 4 as written.

TANGY WHOLE RED LENTILS

Khatte Masoor Dal

WEST AND CENTRAL INDIA

VEGETARIAN
EGG-FREE
GLUTEN-FREE
PEANUT-FREE
SOY-FREE

SERVES 4 ◆ PREP TIME: 15 MINUTES ◆ COOK TIME: 1½ TO 2 HOURS *In most vegetarian homes across India, lentils are a major source of protein and iron. This tangy whole red lentil dish is packed with inexpensive yet filling protein, and makes a tasty, wholesome accompaniment to rice. I really like eating this dal over steaming basmati rice with a little ghee to garnish it with creaminess.*

1 cup whole red lentils (masoor dal)
2½ cups water, divided
½ teaspoon turmeric powder
Kosher salt
1 tablespoon vegetable oil
1 teaspoon cumin seeds
Pinch asafetida
½ cup finely chopped red onion
1 tablespoon Ginger-Garlic Paste (page 46)
1 teaspoon red chili powder
2 teaspoons ground coriander
1 medium tomato, chopped
1 teaspoon Punjabi Garam Masala (page 45)
¾ cup plain yogurt, well whisked

1 In a large pot over medium heat, mix the lentils, 2 cups of water, and the turmeric, and season with salt. Bring to a boil, then reduce the heat to low and simmer, covered, for 1½ hours, or until the lentils are tender. Stir occasionally so the lentils don't stick to the bottom, and add more water if they do. Set aside.

2 In a medium saucepan, heat the oil over medium heat until it's shimmering. Add the cumin seeds and let them crackle, then stir in the asafetida.

3 Add the onion and sauté until light golden. Add the ginger-garlic paste and cook until aromatic. If the onion and paste begin to stick to the pan, loosen them up by adding a few drops of water and continue stirring.

4 Stir in the chili powder and coriander, and cook for 1 minute. Add the tomato and mash it slightly with the back of your spoon as it cooks. Continue stirring and cooking until the oil starts to separate.

5 Add the cooked lentils, remaining ½ cup water, garam masala, and yogurt. Stir well, season with salt, and bring the mixture to a simmer before serving.

Make It Faster: Cook the lentils with turmeric and kosher salt in the pressure cooker for 15 to 20 minutes at high pressure. Use the quick method to release the pressure. Then follow steps 2 through 5 as written.

Make It Easier: Cook the lentils in the slow cooker with turmeric and kosher salt for 3 hours on High or 6 to 8 hours on Low. Then follow steps 2 through 5 as written.

PUNJABI CHICKPEA CURRY

Chole

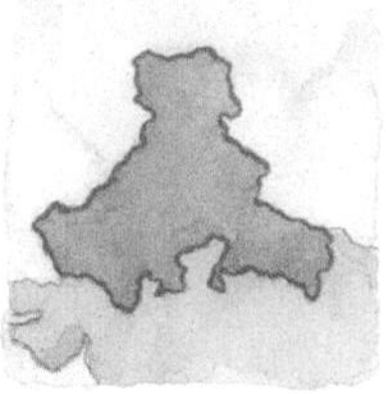

NORTH INDIA

VEGAN
GLUTEN-FREE
PEANUT-FREE
SOY-FREE

SERVES 2 ◆ PREP TIME: 20 MINUTES, PLUS OVERNIGHT TO SOAK ◆ COOK TIME: 1½ HOURS *Chole is a wholesome dish that is traditionally served for breakfast in Chandigarh, along with breads like Amritsari Flatbread (page 94) and slivered onion salad. It is also served as a side dish at lunch or dinner.*

FOR THE ROASTED SPICE BLEND

1 black cardamom pod
1 (1-inch) cinnamon stick
1 Indian bay leaf or Mediterranean bay leaf
5 peppercorns
2 teaspoons cumin seeds
3 teaspoons coriander seeds
1 teaspoon fennel seeds
2 dried Kashmiri chiles

FOR THE CHOLE

1 cup dried chickpeas (channa dal) or one 15-ounce can cooked chickpeas, drained and rinsed
½ teaspoon turmeric powder
2 cups water
Kosher salt
2 tablespoons vegetable oil
1 medium red onion, finely chopped
1 teaspoon Ginger-Garlic Paste (page 46)
2 large tomatoes, chopped
1 teaspoon dried raw mango powder (amchur)
2 small Indian or Thai green chiles, split in half
2 tablespoons minced cilantro leaves and tender stems

To make the roasted spice blend

1 Heat a medium cast-iron skillet over medium heat until hot but not yet smoking. Add all the ingredients for the spice blend and dry roast until the spices are fragrant, stirring continuously for about 5 minutes. Remove the skillet from the heat, transfer the mixture to a plate, and allow it to cool.

2 Grind the roasted spice mixture using a mortar and pestle or spice grinder to a fine powder. Set aside.

Make It Faster: Cook the soaked chickpeas at high pressure in the electric pressure cooker with salt, turmeric, and enough water to cover for 3 to 5 minutes. Use the quick method to release the pressure. Follow steps 3 through 5 as written on the next page.

To make the chole

1 Place the dried chickpeas in a large bowl and pour in enough cold water to cover. Let them soak overnight, then drain them and rinse them well.

2 In a large pot, mix the soaked chickpeas with the turmeric and 2 cups of water. Season with salt. Bring to a boil over medium-high heat, then reduce the heat to low and cook, covered, for 1 hour or until the chickpeas are tender.

3 In a medium saucepan, wok, or kadhai, heat the oil over medium heat until it's shimmering. Add the onion and sauté, stirring, until translucent, about 5 minutes. Add the ginger-garlic paste and stir until the raw smell of the paste disappears, about 2 minutes. Add the tomatoes and cook, stirring and mashing the tomatoes with the back of the spoon until the tomatoes break down and the oil separates, about 10 minutes.

4 Add the dried mango powder and chiles. Stir until fragrant, about 1 minute. Add the roasted spice blend and stir until fragrant. Add a few teaspoons of water if the spices stick to the bottom of the pan, as they tend to burn easily. Cook, stirring frequently, for about 5 minutes.

5 Add the boiled chickpeas with about 1 cup of the water they were boiled in (or plain water, if using canned chickpeas). Stir to combine, and simmer for 15 minutes so that the chickpeas absorb the spices. Garnish with the cilantro leaves.

Make It Easier: Cook the soaked chickpeas in the slow cooker with salt, turmeric, and enough water to cover for about 6 hours on Low. Follow steps 3 through 5 as written.

7

VEGAN AND ALLIUM-FREE

CILANTRO FRITTERS

Kothimbir Vadi

WEST AND CENTRAL INDIA

VEGAN
GLUTEN-FREE
SOY-FREE
ALLIUM-FREE

SERVES 3 TO 4 ◆ PREP TIME: 10 MINUTES ◆ COOK TIME: 10 MINUTES

When my garden is overgrown with cilantro (coriander), I love to put it to good use in this simple, nutritious snack. It is a popular dish in West India, and almost all Maharashtrian homes will serve it to you as a quick snack when you visit. The peanuts, chickpea flour, and cilantro form a delicate balance that will keep you coming back for more.

- 1 cup chickpea flour
- 2 cups coarsely chopped cilantro, leaves and tender stems
- Kosher salt
- 1 teaspoon red chili powder
- ¼ teaspoon asafetida
- ¼ teaspoon turmeric powder
- 2 tablespoons roasted, crushed peanuts
- ½ cup water
- 2 tablespoons vegetable oil, divided

1 In a large bowl, mix together the chickpea flour, cilantro, a pinch of salt, chili powder, asafetida, turmeric, and peanuts. Slowly pour in the water while continuously stirring with a fork or whisk, until a thick batter forms.

2 Coat a microwave-safe glass bowl or plate with 1 teaspoon oil. Transfer the batter to the plate and cover with a lid or another inverted plate. Microwave the plated mixture for 4 minutes on High in a 1,350-watt microwave or a little longer in microwaves with lower wattages.

3 Transfer the microwaved cake to a cutting board and cut into 1-inch squares, bars, or diamond shapes. If you plan to make this earlier, the squares can be refrigerated for up to a week before frying.

4 Heat the remaining oil in a nonstick skillet over medium heat until it's shimmering. Slide in the fritters gently and fry until crisp on the outside, about 30 seconds on each side. Remove and drain on paper towels. Serve with spiced tomato sauce, Sweet and Sour Tamarind Chutney (page 109), or Roasted Green Chile Chutney (page 116) as a snack.

Make It Healthier: You can eat the microwaved fritters without frying. They're just as delicious and lower in fat.

PEANUT AND COCONUT SNACK

Verkadalai Sundal

SOUTH INDIA

FESTIVAL FOOD

VEGAN
GLUTEN-FREE
SOY-FREE
ALLIUM-FREE

SERVES 2 ◆ PREP TIME: 10 MINUTES ◆ COOK TIME: 10 MINUTES *During the Indian festival of Navratri, many Hindu communities across the country fast for nine days. During this type of fast, they don't give up food entirely but can eat only certain foods, such as this allium-free dish. This peanut-based snack is made with fresh or boiled peanuts and is mildly spiced with fresh green chile and ginger.*

1 green chile, split in half lengthwise
1 (½-inch) piece fresh ginger
1 ½ teaspoons vegetable oil
1 teaspoon black mustard seeds
1 teaspoon husked black lentils (urad dal)
Pinch asafetida
10 curry leaves (optional)
1 dried red chile, seeded and torn (optional)
2 cups fresh raw peanuts, boiled for about 5 minutes in salted water
3 tablespoons fresh, or frozen and thawed, grated coconut
Freshly squeezed lemon juice
Fresh cilantro leaves, for garnish (optional)
Kosher salt

1 Using a mortar and pestle, grind the chile and ginger together until they form a thick paste. Set aside.

2 In a saucepan or kadhai, heat the oil on medium until it's shimmering. Add the mustard seeds, and when they crackle, add the split lentils and stir.

3 Reduce the heat to low and when the lentils begin browning, add the asafetida, curry leaves, and chile (if using). Stir briefly and add the crushed chile and ginger mix. Sauté for about 30 seconds, until the rawness of the chile is gone. Add the peanuts and toss until coated with the spiced oil. Sauté for 1 minute.

4 Turn off the heat and add the coconut, mixing well. Transfer to a serving bowl. Garnish with lemon juice and cilantro leaves (if using). Serve immediately.

Substitution Tip: Use cooked kidney beans, chickpeas, or even corn instead of the peanuts.

CABBAGE AND CARROT STIR-FRY

Cabbage and Carrot Thoran

SOUTH INDIA

VEGAN
GLUTEN-FREE
PEANUT-FREE
SOY-FREE
ALLIUM-FREE

SERVES 2 • PREP TIME: 15 MINUTES • COOK TIME: 15 MINUTES *In Kerala, a* thoran *refers to a style of preparing vegetables that uses minimal spices, unlike other heavily-spiced curries. This quick recipe is a nutritious and tasty way to add vegetables to any meal.*

- 2 tablespoons coconut oil or vegetable oil
- 1 teaspoon black mustard seeds
- 1 teaspoon husked black lentils (urad dal)
- 10 to 12 curry leaves (optional)
- 3 green chiles, split in half lengthwise, stemmed
- ½ teaspoon turmeric powder
- Pinch asafetida
- ½ teaspoon ground cumin
- 1 cup finely sliced cabbage
- 1 cup finely grated carrots
- ¼ cup fresh, or frozen and thawed, grated coconut
- Kosher salt

1 In a medium saucepan or kadhai, heat the oil over medium-high heat until it's shimmering. Reduce the heat to medium and add the mustard seeds, allowing them to crackle. Add the black lentils and allow them to pop and change color slightly.

2 Add the curry leaves (if using) and chiles, and stir until fragrant, about 15 seconds. Add the turmeric, asafetida, and cumin, and stir vigorously to ensure that the spices don't burn and the oil turns yellow, about 10 seconds.

3 Add the cabbage and carrots and continue stirring until they start to wilt, about 1 minute. Cover and let the cabbage and carrots steam, stirring occasionally, until wilted, 7 to 10 minutes. Remove the lid and turn the heat up, cooking the cabbage and carrots until any remaining water is evaporated. When dry, add the grated coconut and stir until it's nicely mixed into the cabbage, about 1 minute.

4 Season with salt and serve hot with rice or any Indian bread.

Substitution Tip: Use vegetables you have on hand, such as shredded beets, green beans, and shredded winter squash. Follow the same method, taking care to cut the vegetables small so that they cook quickly.

SPICED FRIED EGGPLANT

Baigun Bhaaja

EAST INDIA

VEGAN
GLUTEN-FREE
PEANUT-FREE
SOY-FREE
ALLIUM-FREE

SERVES 2 ◆ PREP TIME: 10 MINUTES ◆ COOK TIME: 10 TO 12 MINUTES

This simple eggplant dish from West Bengal is mild on the spice. With just two steps and four ingredients, this dish is as simple to prepare as it is satisfying. I recommend having it as a side vegetable dish or even as an appetizer.

1 large dark eggplant
1 to 2 teaspoons turmeric powder
1 teaspoon red chili powder
Kosher salt
Oil, for shallow frying

1 Cut the eggplant into circles about 1 inch thick. Toss with the turmeric and chili powder. Season with salt. Set aside for 5 minutes.

2 In a skillet or a nonstick frying pan, heat the oil over medium heat until it's shimmering. Working in batches, gently slide two to three eggplant slices into the hot oil. Fry for 2 to 3 minutes on each side until cooked through and browned. To check for doneness, insert a fork into the eggplant; if it goes through easily, the eggplant is cooked. Remove and drain on a plate lined with paper towels. Repeat until all the eggplant is fried. Serve hot.

Serving Tip: If you plan to serve this as an appetizer, try a mustard dipping sauce or plain yogurt seasoned with salt and some Roasted Cumin Powder (page 42).

CRUNCHY OKRA

Kurkuri Bhindi

WEST AND CENTRAL INDIA

VEGAN
GLUTEN-FREE
PEANUT-FREE
SOY-FREE
ALLIUM-FREE

SERVES 2 ◆ PREP TIME: 10 MINUTES, PLUS 1½ HOURS TO DRY AND MARINATE ◆ COOK TIME: 10 TO 15 MINUTES *If you have avoided okra all your life due to its stickiness, this dish from Gujarat will completely change your mind. I always make a little extra because past experience has taught me that these crunchy morsels disappear quite quickly. This is a great dish for the vegan diet.*

- 9 ounces okra, stemmed, cut into thin strips
- ½ teaspoon turmeric powder
- 1 teaspoon Coriander-Cumin Spice Blend (page 43)
- 2 teaspoons red chili powder
- Pinch asafetida
- 1 teaspoon powdered sugar (optional)
- ½ teaspoon chaat masala (optional)
- ½ teaspoon dried raw mango powder (amchur)
- 1 teaspoon Basic Homemade Garam Masala (page 44)
- 1½ tablespoons chickpea flour
- Kosher salt
- Vegetable oil, for deep frying

1 Using a clean towel, completely dry the okra and place it in the sun for 1 hour.

2 In a large bowl, mix the okra, turmeric, coriander-cumin blend, chili powder, asafetida, powdered sugar (if using), chaat masala (if using), mango powder, garam masala, and chickpea flour. Season with salt and mix well. Leave on the counter at room temperature for 30 minutes.

3 In a deep frying pan, wok, or kadhai, heat the oil until it's shimmering. Working in batches, add the okra to the oil and fry until crispy. Remove from the oil using a slotted cooking spoon and place on a plate lined with paper towels. Continue until all the okra is fried. Serve hot with Indian breads or as an appetizer.

Serving Tip: While you fry the batches of okra, do not put the hot crispy finished okra in a covered container. This will make it steam and destroy all the crispiness.

TANGY STIR-FRIED RADISH

Muji Kael

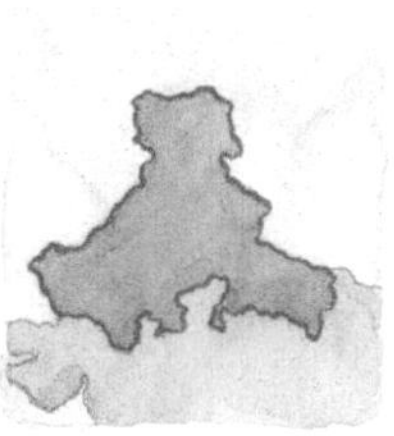

NORTH INDIA

FESTIVAL FOOD

VEGAN
GLUTEN-FREE
PEANUT-FREE
SOY-FREE
ALLIUM-FREE

SERVES 2 ◆ PREP TIME: 15 MINUTES ◆ COOK TIME: 10 MINUTES *Here, the long and thick daikon radish is transformed into something delicious and unexpected. Kashmir is the land of the famous Wazwan, a 36-course meal, in which the Kashmiri Pandit community uses uncommon vegetables like radishes, lotus roots, kohlrabis, morel mushrooms, and various greens. Muji kael is an important dish, prepared and distributed to family members during the festival of Shivratri.*

1½ teaspoons carom seeds
2 whole cloves
1 pound daikon radish
½ cup vegetable oil
1½ teaspoons cumin seeds
Pinch asafetida
1½ teaspoons Kashmiri red chili powder
1 tablespoon water
1 tablespoon ground fennel
1 teaspoon ground dried ginger
1 black cardamom pod
Kosher salt
1½ teaspoons dried raw mango powder (amchur), or the juice of 2 large limes or 1 lemon, or 3 tablespoons tamarind paste diluted in about 2 tablespoons water

1 In a mortar, combine the carom seeds and cloves. Pound with the pestle until powdered. Set aside.

2 Cut the radish into long, slender strips the size of French fries. In a deep frying pan, saucepan, or kadhai, heat the oil on medium-high until it is almost smoking. Turn the heat down to low and deep fry the radish pieces until crisp. Remove using a slotted spoon and drain on a plate lined with paper towels. continued ▸

3 Remove all but 2 tablespoons of oil from the pan and place the pan back on low heat. Add the cumin, the carom and clove mixture, and the asafetida. Stir for 30 seconds, until fragrant. Add the chili powder and 1 tablespoon of water so that the spices do not burn, stirring continuously for about 30 seconds.

4 Add the fennel, ginger, black cardamom, salt, and radish pieces and stir to combine. Add the dried mango powder (or lime juice, lemon juice, or tamarind paste) and mix well, stirring frequently until the liquid has dried up completely. Serve hot with white rice and dal, or with any Indian breads.

Cooking Tip: Use Kashmiri red chili powder if you can find it, as it adds a lovely red hue to the dish.

EGGLESS OMELET

Besan Cheela

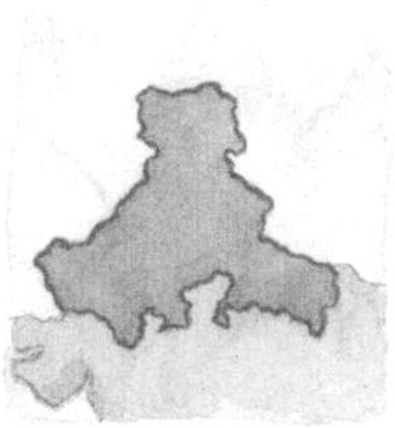

NORTH INDIA

VEGAN
GLUTEN-FREE
PEANUT-FREE
SOY-FREE
ALLIUM-FREE

SERVES 2 ◆ PREP TIME: 10 MINUTES ◆ COOK TIME: 10 MINUTES *Held together by chickpea flour, this eggless omelet from Rajasthan can be filled with your favorite vegetables. You can get creative with the fillings or have the basic version, which will take just a few minutes to cook. Either way, it's a great way to start the day, or for a light snack.*

1 cup chickpea flour (besan)
1 green chile, seeded and chopped
¼ teaspoon red chili powder
¼ teaspoon freshly ground black pepper
½ teaspoon ground coriander
2 teaspoons chopped cilantro leaves
1 tablespoon chopped tomato (optional)
½ cup water
1 teaspoon vegetable oil
Kosher salt

1 In a large mixing bowl, add the chickpea flour, chile, chili powder, pepper, coriander, cilantro, and chopped tomato (if using), along with the water. If needed, add up to ¼ cup more water to create a batter with a pourable consistency, similar to pancake batter.

2 In a nonstick frying pan or skillet, heat the oil over medium-low heat, swirling it around in the pan to cover its surface. When hot, add a ladleful of the batter and swirl in the pan to make an even round. Cover the pan and cook until the omelet is set and small brown dots appear on the bottom, about 40 seconds. (Check by slightly lifting the omelet.) Flip the omelet, and continue cooking on the other side until small brown dots appear on the bottom. Repeat until you have used up all the batter, adding more oil before cooking each one; you should have 4 to 6 cheelas. Serve warm with Roasted Green Chile Chutney (page 116) or ketchup.

Make It Healthier: Add vegetables and other ingredients to the omelet by mixing them into the batter in step 1. I enjoy grated vegan cheese, grated cauliflower, and herbs such as mint or basil.

Serving Tip: Keep the cheelas warm in an Indian roti box or in a covered serving dish until you're ready to eat.

DEEP-FRIED PANCAKES

Dhuska

WEST AND CENTRAL INDIA

FESTIVAL FOOD

VEGAN
GLUTEN-FREE
PEANUT-FREE
SOY-FREE
ALLIUM-FREE

MAKES 15 TO 18 PANCAKES ◆ PREP TIME: 15 MINUTES, PLUS OVERNIGHT TO SOAK ◆ COOK TIME: 10 MINUTES *This rice and chickpea flour pancake from Jharkhand has a texture like a soft pancake with a crispy edge. Traditionally, the aroma of these pancakes fills the air during the Hindu festivals of Holi and Durga Puja. I like adding freshly cooked peas or even herbs to my batter to make these even more interesting.*

1 cup white rice
1 cup split yellow chickpeas (channa dal)
1 green chile, stemmed and seeded
1 (½-inch) piece fresh ginger
1 teaspoon cumin seeds (optional)
½ teaspoon turmeric powder
2 tablespoons finely chopped cilantro leaves
Kosher salt
Vegetable oil, for deep frying

1 Put the rice and chickpeas in a large bowl. Cover with water by at least 1 inch. Soak overnight at room temperature.

2 The next morning, strain the chickpeas and rice, reserving the soaking water. In a spice grinder or blender, grind the rice and chickpeas with the chile, ginger, and cumin seeds (if using), adding the soaking water as needed while grinding to make the batter smooth, similar to pancake batter. The batter should be ground fine so there is no grit when you rub it between your fingers. Transfer to a bowl and add the turmeric and cilantro. Season with salt.

3 In a deep frying pan or saucepan, heat a couple of inches of oil over medium heat for deep frying. When the oil shimmers, pour several small ladlefuls of batter, each about 3 inches in diameter, into the oil. Turn once or twice while frying to promote even browning. Remove from the oil using a slotted spoon and place on a plate lined with paper towels. Serve hot with Roasted Green Chile Chutney (page 116) or Amritsari Flatbread (page 94).

Make It Healthier: You can also fry these pancakes in just a few tablespoons of oil, more like a Western breakfast pancake.

COCONUT RICE

Thengai Sadam

SOUTH INDIA

VEGAN
GLUTEN-FREE
SOY-FREE
PEANUT-FREE
ALLIUM-FREE

SERVES 2 ◆ PREP TIME: 10 MINUTES ◆ COOK TIME: 10 MINUTES *The southern states of India are blessed with endless lines of coconut palms. This recipe is made in the homes of Tamil Brahmins, a Tamil Nadu community famed for its variety of vegetarian dishes and, more important, its range of allium-free dishes due to religious beliefs. It's very subtly spiced and has lovely texture because of the cashews.*

- 1 tablespoon coconut oil or vegetable oil
- 1 teaspoon black mustard seeds
- 1½ teaspoons split yellow chickpeas (channa dal)
- 2 teaspoons husked black lentils (urad dal)
- 2 dried red chiles, broken into pieces
- 2 green chiles, split in half lengthwise
- 1 (½-inch) piece fresh ginger, slivered (optional)
- Pinch asafetida
- 12 curry leaves (optional)
- 8 to 10 cashews
- 1 cup fresh, or frozen and thawed, grated coconut flesh
- Kosher salt
- 2 cups cooked and cooled white rice

1 In a wide frying pan, kadhai, or wok, heat the oil over medium heat. Add the mustard seeds, and when they crackle, add the chickpeas. Stir until the chickpeas start to change color. Turn the heat to low, add the lentils and red chiles, and keep frying and stirring until the dals change color. Remove the red chile pieces and reserve.

2 Add the green chiles, ginger (if using), asafetida, curry leaves (if using), and cashews. Continue stirring and frying until the cashews are lightly browned.

3 Add back the red chiles, along with the grated coconut flesh. Season with salt. Fry this mixture until the coconut turns light brown. Add the rice and mix well. Serve with poppadums, Cooling Yogurt and Vegetable Salad (page 104), or on its own.

Cooking Tip: If you don't have leftover rice, cook basmati rice and allow it to cool thoroughly by spreading it out on a plate. This will also help the grains stay separate.

8

POULTRY AND MEAT

TANDOORI CHICKEN

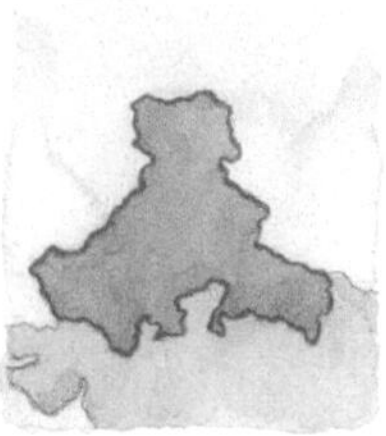

NORTH INDIA

EGG-FREE
GLUTEN-FREE
PEANUT-FREE
SOY-FREE

SERVES 4 ◆ PREP TIME: 20 MINUTES, PLUS 6 HOURS TO OVERNIGHT TO MARINATE ◆ COOK TIME: 45 MINUTES *Tandoori chicken is arguably India's most popular culinary gift to the world. It gets its name from the tandoor, or clay oven, in which it is cooked. I think the closest you can get to the taste of the authentic smoky Tandoori chicken is to use a coal-fired barbeque, but a regular oven will also do a good job.*

FOR THE FIRST MARINADE

4 whole chicken legs (skin on)
1 teaspoon turmeric powder
2 teaspoons red chili powder
Kosher salt
1 tablespoon freshly squeezed lime juice

FOR THE SECOND MARINADE

2½ tablespoons Ginger-Garlic Paste (page 46)
1 cup plain yogurt, whisked until smooth
1 tablespoon Roasted Cumin Powder (page 42)
1 teaspoon freshly ground black pepper
2 teaspoons Punjabi Garam Masala (page 45)
1 tablespoon dried fenugreek leaves
3 to 4 drops red food coloring
3 tablespoons vegetable oil or melted ghee for basting

To make the first marinade

1 Score the chicken skin and flesh at an angle so the marinade can penetrate the flesh.

2 In a large bowl, mix the turmeric, chili powder, salt, and lime juice. Using your hands, rub this mixture on the chicken legs. Set aside for at least 30 minutes. If longer than 30 minutes, refrigerate until you are ready to proceed.

To make the second marinade

1 After the first marinade, in another bowl, mix the ginger-garlic paste, yogurt, cumin, pepper, garam masala, fenugreek leaves, and red food coloring.

2 Using your hands, rub this into the chicken. Marinate for at least 5 hours or overnight, covered, in the refrigerator.

3 Remove the chicken from the refrigerator and set aside at room temperature for 30 minutes.

4 Preheat the oven to 350°F.

5 Arrange the chicken legs on a wire rack over a baking pan and place in the oven.

6 Cook the legs at least 15 minutes on one side. Remove the pan from the oven, turn the legs over, and baste with ghee or oil. After 15 minutes, repeat the process, turning and basting again. Continue to cook for another 15 minutes, or until the legs are well-browned and the juices run clear. Remove from the oven and serve hot with Roasted Green Chile Chutney (page 116), onion rings, and lime wedges.

Substitution Tip: To make lamb tandoori, simply substitute 8 lamb chops for the chicken (2 per serving), and marinate them the first time in an airtight container for at least 1 hour or overnight. Grill the lamb chops for 8 to 10 minutes per side, or roast them in the oven at 400°F for 10 to 12 minutes, or until an instant-read thermometer inserted into the meatiest part of a chop registers at least 145°F.

CHICKEN BRAISED IN SPICES AND GHEE

Chicken Ghee Roast

SOUTH INDIA

EGG-FREE
GLUTEN-FREE
PEANUT-FREE
SOY-FREE

SERVES 4 ♦ PREP TIME: 15 MINUTES, PLUS 2 HOURS TO OVERNIGHT TO MARINATE ♦ COOK TIME: 30 MINUTES Ghee roast *is a term used for a thick gravy dish that is braised in ghee, or clarified butter. It has little to do with roasting as a process. Since the spices are first fried in ghee and then ground to a paste, they tend to be more aromatic, and the resulting masala or masala paste is creamy and has many layers of flavor.*

- ¾ cup plain yogurt
- 1½ teaspoons freshly squeezed lime juice
- 1 teaspoon turmeric powder
- 1 tablespoon kosher salt
- 1 teaspoon freshly ground black pepper
- 4 whole chicken legs
- 4 tablespoons plus 1 teaspoon ghee, divided
- 6 garlic cloves
- 6 dried red Kashmiri chiles
- 1 tablespoon coriander seeds
- ¼ teaspoon fenugreek seeds
- 1 teaspoon cumin seeds
- 1 cup water

1 In a large bowl, mix the yogurt, lime juice, turmeric, salt, and pepper. Add the chicken and coat thoroughly. Cover the bowl and refrigerate for at least 2 hours or overnight.

2 Remove the chicken from the refrigerator.

3 In a cast-iron skillet or kadhai, melt 2 tablespoons of the ghee over medium heat until it's shimmering. Add the garlic, chiles, coriander, fenugreek and cumin, and cook, stirring constantly, until fragrant, about 5 minutes. Remove the skillet from the heat and allow the mixture to cool.

4 Transfer the spices to a blender, spice grinder, or mortar and pestle, and grind into a fine paste, adding a few drops of water at a time to aid the grinding. Remember that there is ghee in this mixture, which does not mix well with water, so use only a tiny quantity of water to loosen the paste, if required.

5 In the same cast-iron skillet or kadhai you used for cooking the spices, melt the remaining 2 tablespoons plus 1 teaspoon ghee over medium heat until it's shimmering. Let the excess marinade drip from the chicken, then gently slide the chicken pieces into the ghee and fry them until lightly browned, about 5 minutes on each side.

6 Make a clearing in the center of the pan between the chicken pieces and add the masala paste. Stir the paste in that space until fragrant, about 5 minutes, then move the chicken pieces to the center of the pan and turn them to coat in the paste. Mix thoroughly and add 1 cup of water to the pan. Reduce the heat to low and cook until most of the water has evaporated and an instant-read thermometer inserted into the meatiest part of a chicken leg registers 170°F, about 10 minutes more. Serve hot with Plain Basmati Rice (page 76) or Easy Rice and Lentil Crêpes (page 97).

Cooking Tip: Ghee roasts taste even better the next day, when the spices and ghee have had a chance to get to know each other better.

Substitution Tip: Make this vegetarian by omitting the chicken and using about 1 pound paneer cubes. The marinating time will be 20 minutes, and you'll need about 10 minutes cooking time.

PEPPER CHICKEN

Chettinad Milagu Kozhi Varuval

SOUTH INDIA

EGG-FREE
DAIRY-FREE
GLUTEN-FREE
PEANUT-FREE
SOY-FREE

SERVES 4 ◆ PREP TIME: 15 MINUTES, PLUS 1 HOUR TO MARINATE ◆ COOK TIME: 30 MINUTES *Chettinad cuisine, from South India, is perhaps the most aromatic and spiciest of all Indian cuisines. Though it can be incredibly hot, I love the bold flavors of Chettinad food, and between glasses of chilled water will shamelessly help myself to seconds. The combination of chicken and pepper in this recipe makes it a very potent remedy for colds.*

- 3 teaspoons Ginger-Garlic Paste (page 46), divided
- 3 teaspoons freshly ground black pepper, divided
- 1 tablespoon ground coriander
- 2 teaspoons red chili powder
- Kosher salt
- 1 pound bone-in chicken legs and thighs, cut into medium pieces (skin on)
- 2 tablespoons vegetable or coconut oil
- 3 (1-inch) cinnamon sticks
- 3 whole cloves
- 3 to 4 green cardamom pods
- 3 Indian bay leaves or Mediterranean bay leaves
- 1 teaspoon fennel seeds
- 10 curry leaves (optional)
- 1 cup finely chopped red onion
- 2 finely chopped tomatoes
- ½ cup water
- Juice of 1 lime
- 1 tablespoon chopped cilantro leaves and stems

1 In a small bowl, mix together 1½ teaspoons of ginger-garlic paste, 1½ teaspoons of pepper, the coriander, and the chili powder. Season with salt. Place the chicken pieces in a large bowl and, using your hands, rub this marinade all over the chicken. Cover the bowl and refrigerate for at least 1 hour.

2 In a heavy saucepan or kadhai, heat the oil over medium heat until it's shimmering. Turn the heat to low and add the cinnamon, cloves, cardamom pods, bay leaves, fennel seeds, and curry leaves (if using). Stir until fragrant, about 1 minute.

3 Add the onion and sauté until softened and light brown. If the onion is browning too fast without softening, add a few drops of water to reduce the temperature and continue frying.

4 Add the remaining 1½ teaspoons of ginger-garlic paste and stir until fragrant. Add the tomatoes and mash with the back of the spoon as they cook to make a paste, about 5 minutes. Add ½ cup of water, cover, and allow the masala to cook for 5 to 7 minutes. The oil will start to separate and float to the top when it is ready.

5 When the oil in the masala paste has begun to separate, add the marinated chicken pieces. Turn the heat to medium-low and cook the chicken for about 15 minutes, or until an instant-read thermometer inserted into the meatiest piece registers 165°F. Stir in between the chicken pieces, and add a little water at a time to ensure that the chicken cooks evenly. You don't want a gravy consistency, as this is a dry dish when finished.

6 When the chicken is tender, garnish with the remaining 1½ teaspoons of pepper, the lime juice, and the cilantro leaves. Serve hot with Plain Basmati Rice (page 76), Easy Rice and Lentil Crêpes (page 97), or roti.

Substitution Tip: Make this dish vegan by adding button mushrooms instead of chicken. Marinate the mushrooms for 10 minutes and cook them in the finished masala paste for 5 to 10 minutes.

Cooking Tip: Reduce the amount of chili pepper if you like, but do not reduce the amount of black pepper, as the combination of pepper, chicken, and whole spices is what makes this dish unique.

MURGH TIKKA MASALA

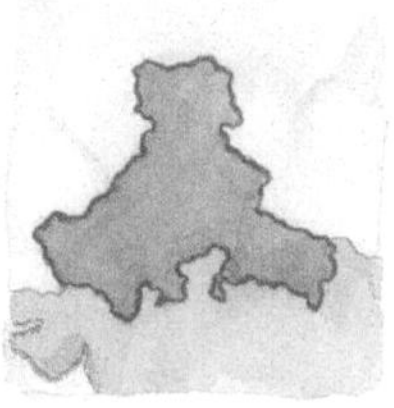

NORTH INDIA

EGG-FREE
PEANUT-FREE
SOY-FREE

SERVES 4 • PREP TIME: 20 MINUTES • COOK TIME: 45 MINUTES *The first Indian dish that people from outside of India tell me they love is chicken tikka masala. This is a Punjabi version, where leftover tandoori chicken is engulfed in rich gravy. The flavor of the tandoori chicken adds a lot of depth to the resulting gravy. You can use takeout tandoori chicken—just debone it.*

- 3 tablespoons vegetable oil
- 2 medium red onions, puréed coarsely in a blender
- 1 tablespoon minced garlic
- 2 teaspoons ground coriander
- 2 teaspoons red chili powder
- ½ teaspoon turmeric powder
- ¾ cup tomato purée
- 10 cashews, soaked in water for 10 minutes, then drained and puréed
- ½ cup plain yogurt
- 2 Indian bay leaves or Mediterranean bay leaves
- 1 tablespoon grated fresh ginger
- 1 green chile, chopped
- 1 teaspoon Basic Homemade Garam Masala (page 44)
- Kosher salt
- 2 cups water
- 3 cups boneless chicken tandoori
- 1 tablespoon crushed, dried fenugreek leaves (kastoori methi) (optional)
- ½ cup cream
- 2 tablespoons chopped cilantro leaves

1 Heat the oil in a medium saucepan or kadhai over high heat until it is shimmering. Add the puréed onions and garlic and sauté. The onions will let out a lot of water for about 5 minutes. Keep the flame high and dry them out. When the water has evaporated, turn the heat to medium and let the onions cook for 8 to 9 minutes, until they are light brown.

2 Reduce the heat to low and add the coriander, chili powder, and turmeric. Stir to mix with the onions and cook for about 30 seconds.

3 Add the tomato and cashew purées, then the yogurt; mix well. Cook for about 10 minutes, until the oil starts to separate and the mixture is fairly dry. Add the bay leaves, ginger, chile, and garam masala. Season with salt, and stir for about 2 minutes.

4 Add the water, cover, and cook about 15 minutes, stirring occasionally. Stir in the chicken and dried fenugreek (if using). Add the cream and cook another 5 minutes. Garnish with cilantro leaves and more cream, if desired. Serve with Amritsari Flatbread (page 94) or Aromatic Yellow Rice (page 77).

Ingredient Tip: Dried fenugreek leaves are always added toward the end of the cooking process and give the dish a lovely aroma and flavor.

Cooking Tip: If you plan to serve the dish later, add the cream when you are reheating it, or the cream will break apart.

PORK VINDALOO

WEST AND CENTRAL INDIA

FESTIVAL FOOD

EGG-FREE
DAIRY-FREE
GLUTEN-FREE
PEANUT-FREE
SOY-FREE

SERVES 2 ◆ PREP TIME: 20 MINUTES ◆ COOK TIME: 1 HOUR, 20 MINUTES

The sun-drenched state of Goa is famous for this fiery pork delicacy, which is a legacy of Portuguese rule in the land. Sharp coconut or palm vinegar ages this striking red dish and makes it taste better over a few days. It's sometimes doused with a little alcohol like Feni, a local Goan cashew-based drink, or rum. It's a traditional favorite for the festive Christmas table, and I usually make it a couple of days early so that any fat in the dish has time to render and mature in flavor.

1 pound boneless pork shoulder, with fat and skin, cut into 1-inch cubes
Kosher salt
2 teaspoons turmeric powder, divided
15 dried Kashmiri chiles
2 teaspoons whole cumin seeds, dry roasted
2 (1-inch) cinnamon sticks, divided
10 peppercorns, divided
7 whole cloves, divided
1 teaspoon sugar
10 garlic cloves, coarsely chopped
1 (1-inch) piece fresh ginger, peeled and coarsely chopped
½ cup palm vinegar, coconut vinegar, or white vinegar
1 medium red onion, coarsely chopped
1½ tablespoons vegetable oil
1 cup water

1 In a large bowl, season the pork with salt. Add 1 teaspoon of turmeric and mix well, using your hands, to work the spice into the meat. Cover and refrigerate for at least 15 minutes while you prepare the masala paste. If you have time, you could leave it overnight.

2 Using a spice grinder, food processor, or mortar and pestle, mix the dried chiles, roasted cumin seeds, remaining teaspoon of turmeric, 1 piece of cinnamon, 5 peppercorns, 4 whole cloves, and the sugar. Grind until the spices are a fine powder. Add the garlic, ginger, and vinegar and continue grinding to a fine paste. Transfer the paste to a small bowl. Set aside.

3 Add the onion to the grinder, food processor, or mortar and pestle and pulse or grind once or twice. Do not rinse out the container.

4 In a large saucepan, heat the oil over medium heat until it's shimmering. Add the mashed onion, the remaining 5 peppercorns, the remaining piece of cinnamon, and the remaining 3 whole cloves. Cook, stirring constantly, until the onion is soft and fragrant, about 5 minutes.

5 Add the masala paste and cook, stirring occasionally, until the oil separates and the mixture starts to sizzle, about 5 minutes.

6 Add the pork and cook, stirring occasionally, until browned, about 10 minutes. Add 1 cup of water to the food processor, spice grinder, or mortar bowl, and swirl to rinse. Pour this mixture into the pan and bring to a simmer, stirring occasionally. Reduce the heat to maintain a gentle simmer, cover, and cook until the pork is fork tender, about 1 hour.

7 Serve immediately with rice or Goan Fermented Steamed Buns (page 100). Or, for better flavor, cool and store overnight or for up to 2 days in a sealed container in the refrigerator, and reheat well before serving.

Make It Faster: To use an Instant Pot electric pressure cooker, follow steps 1 through 3 as is. Starting with step 4, use the Sauté setting. Once the water and spice mixture is added to the pork in step 6, set it to Meat Stew for approximately 7 to 10 minutes. After another 5 minutes, release the remaining pressure using the quick method. Check the tenderness of the meat.

Make It Easier: To make this in a slow cooker, follow steps 1 through 5 using a saucepan. Brown the pork as instructed in step 6 and transfer the mixture to the slow cooker. Add ½ cup more liquid and cook on Low for 4 hours. Check to see if the pork is tender (different cuts and the amount of fat may affect the cook time). If not, cook on Low for another 1 hour. If the sauce is too runny, reduce the gravy in a saucepan on the stove.

NAGA PORK WITH BAMBOO SHOOTS

Thevo Chu

NORTHEAST INDIA

EGG-FREE
DAIRY-FREE
GLUTEN-FREE
PEANUT-FREE
SOY-FREE

SERVES 2 • PREP TIME: 10 MINUTES • COOK TIME: 40 TO 50 MINUTES

The cuisine of Nagaland is heavily influenced by its tribal communities and very different from other Indian cuisines in that it uses more fresh herbs and spices and very little cooking oil. This not only makes the food healthier but also gives it a whole new dimension of flavors in the larger context of the subcontinent's cuisine.

1 pound boneless pork shoulder, with fat, cut into small cubes
1 teaspoon vegetable oil (optional)
Kosher salt
¼ cup finely sliced fermented bamboo shoots
1 tablespoon finely chopped fresh ginger
2 tablespoons finely chopped garlic
3 teaspoons red chili powder or 5 whole red chiles
½ to ¾ cup water

1 In a saucepan over medium heat, add the pork and render it in the heat for a few minutes. If desired, add a teaspoon of oil to start the process. Season with salt and add enough water to cover the pork. Bring the water to a boil, reduce the heat, and simmer the pork for 30 minutes, until it is about half cooked.

2 Add the bamboo shoots along with their juices and continue stirring the pork mixture until the water is nearly evaporated, about 15 minutes.

3 Add the ginger, garlic, and chili powder and stir for 2 to 3 minutes. Add ½ to ¾ cup more water and bring to a boil for an additional 5 minutes to form a medium-thick curry. Serve hot with rice.

Ingredient Tip: Fermented bamboo shoots are the edible shoots of the bamboo plant, and they usually come packed in jars or cans with brining liquid. You can find them in Chinese or Indian supermarkets, or online.

SWEET, TANGY, AND SAVORY STEWED PORK

Mangalore Pork Indad

SOUTH INDIA

FESTIVAL FOOD

EGG-FREE
DAIRY-FREE
GLUTEN-FREE
PEANUT-FREE
SOY-FREE

SERVES 4 ◆ PREP TIME: 20 MINUTES, PLUS 30 MINUTES TO MARINATE ◆ COOK TIME: 1 HOUR, 15 MINUTES *This traditional Mangalorean recipe marries sweet, hot, spicy, and tangy to give the pork a wonderful flavor that deepens as it matures over a few days. Like all Indian-Catholic pork dishes, this one benefits from the layer of rendered fat that emerges on top of the dish after cooking. It makes its appearance during Easter and christenings and is lovingly fussed over by the women of the family until the balance of all four flavors is perfect.*

2 pounds boneless pork shoulder, with fat and skin, cut into small cubes
6 garlic cloves, minced
1 tablespoon minced ginger
1 tablespoon Ginger-Garlic Paste (page 46)
¼ teaspoon turmeric powder
¼ teaspoon red chili powder
Kosher salt
10 peppercorns
2 whole cloves
1 (1-inch) cinnamon stick
½ teaspoon poppy seeds
10 dried red Kashmiri chiles
2 teaspoons cumin seeds
1 medium red onion, finely chopped
1½ teaspoons raisins
1 tablespoon tamarind paste
2 garlic cloves
¼ cup palm vinegar, coconut vinegar, or white vinegar
2 tablespoons vegetable oil
1 cup water
½ teaspoon sugar

1 In a large bowl, mix together the pork, minced garlic, ginger, ginger-garlic paste, turmeric, and chili powder. Using your hands, rub this mixture onto the pork. Season with salt. Cover and set aside. Let the pork marinate for 30 minutes.

2 In a dry, medium cast-iron skillet or tava over low heat, roast the peppercorns, cloves, cinnamon, poppy seeds, chiles, and cumin seeds until fragrant, about 1 minute. Transfer the mixture to a plate to cool, then grind the spices in a spice grinder to a fine powder. Add the onion, raisins, tamarind paste, garlic cloves, and vinegar. Blend until smooth. Set aside. continued ▶

3 In a large, heavy pot with a lid, heat the oil over high heat until it begins to shimmer. Add the pork and let it brown for 2 to 5 minutes, turning occasionally to cook all sides. Take care not to burn the marinade.

4 Reduce the heat to low. Add the masala paste and stir vigorously until the mixture is fragrant and the oil is infused with the red color from the paste, about 10 minutes total.

5 Add the water and the sugar. Bring the liquid to a boil, cover the pot, and cook over medium heat until the pork is very tender, about 1 hour. Check the seasonings and adjust the vinegar-and-sugar balance to your taste. You want all four flavors (spicy, salty, sour, and sweet) to be equally represented in each bite.

6 Serve with Goan Fermented Steamed Buns (page 100) or Plain Basmati Rice (page 76). Or transfer the stewed pork to an airtight container and refrigerate for up to 3 days. (The flavors are even better the next day.) Reheat well before serving.

Make It Faster: Using an Instant Pot electric pressure cooker, follow steps 1 and 2 as written. Follow steps 3 and 4 using the Sauté feature. Set the cooker to Meat Stew for approximately 12 minutes, then release the remaining pressure using the quick method and check the tenderness of the meat. If it's still not tender, cook another 3 minutes and check it again. Keep checking every 3 minutes until it is tender. When I cook this dish in a pressure cooker, the vinegar and sugar flavors are less intense, so check and adjust accordingly before serving.

Make It Easier: Follow steps 1 through 4 as written. After browning the meat and mixing in the spice mixture, transfer everything to a slow cooker. Add 1½ cups water (instead of 1 cup) and cook on Low for 4 hours. Check if the pork is tender (different cuts and the amount of fat may affect cook time). If not, cook on Low for 1 additional hour. If the sauce is too runny, reduce the gravy in a saucepan. When I cook this dish in a slow cooker, the vinegar and sugar flavors are less intense, so check and adjust accordingly before serving.

PORK COOKED IN VINEGAR AND SPICES

Coorgi Pandi Curry

SOUTH INDIA

DAIRY-FREE
EGG-FREE
GLUTEN-FREE
PEANUT-FREE
SOY-FREE

SERVES 4 ◆ PREP TIME: 20 MINUTES, PLUS 20 MINUTES TO MARINATE ◆ COOK TIME: 1 HOUR, 40 MINUTES *Whenever I travel to Coorg in South India, my first task is to order a bowl of Coorgi Pandi Curry. This distinctive dark, rich pork curry uses kachampuli, a local vinegar made from the sour fruit Garcinia gummi-gutta, which grows in the area. My recipe calls for this vinegar, but if you cannot find it, you can use malt vinegar or tamarind paste instead.*

2 teaspoons cumin seeds
½ teaspoon black mustard seeds
2 pounds pork shoulder, with skin and fat, cut into small cubes
1 teaspoon freshly ground black pepper
1 teaspoon turmeric powder
Kosher salt
2 tablespoons sesame oil
2 green chiles, seeded and chopped
1 (2-inch) piece fresh ginger, grated
5 medium red onions, sliced
1 whole garlic head, cloves separated and peeled, coarsely chopped
3 tablespoons ground coriander
1 tablespoon chili powder
½ cup water
1 to 2 tablespoons kachampuli vinegar or 1¼ to 2½ tablespoons malt vinegar or tamarind paste

1 Heat a medium skillet or tava over medium heat. Add the cumin seeds and roast until fragrant. Transfer to a plate to cool. Do the same with the mustard seeds. In a spice grinder or mortar and pestle, grind the cooled seeds into a powder. Set aside.

2 In a large bowl, toss the pork with the pepper and turmeric. Season with salt, cover the bowl, and set aside. Let the pork marinate for 20 minutes.

3 In a medium saucepan or kadhai, heat the sesame oil over medium heat until it's shimmering. Add the chiles, ginger, onions, and garlic. Sauté until the mixture is aromatic and lightly browned. Remove the pan from the heat and scrape the mixture into the bowl with the pork. Toss well to combine. continued ▶

4 In the same saucepan over low heat, mix the ground coriander and chili powder. Stir for about 30 seconds, then add the pork and seasonings from the bowl, along with ½ cup of water. Stir well and cover the pan. Adjust the heat to medium and cook until the water evaporates, 10 to 12 minutes.

5 When all the water has evaporated, add more water to just cover the meat, and cook uncovered over medium heat until the pork is very tender, 45 minutes to 1 hour depending on the thickness of the meat.

6 Add the vinegar or tamarind paste. Stir and cook for another 10 minutes over low heat. The oil should separate and rise to the surface. Taste and adjust the amounts of seasonings and vinegar. Add the ground roasted cumin and mustard seeds to the curry, stir, and cook for another 5 to 10 minutes. Serve with Plain Basmati Rice (page 76) or Easy Rice and Lentil Crêpes (page 97).

Make It Faster: Follow steps 1 and 2 as written. Follow steps 3 and 4 with the Instant Pot electric pressure cooker on Sauté. Then set the cooker to Meat Stew for approximately 7 minutes. Another 5 minutes after that, release the remaining pressure using the quick method and check the tenderness of the meat. If it is still not tender, add another 3 minutes at a time to the cooking time. When the meat is cooked tender, follow step 6 with the lid off and the cooker set to Sauté.

Make It Easier: Follow steps 1 through 4 as written, then transfer everything to your slow cooker. Add 1 cup water instead of ½ cup and cook on Low for 4 to 5 hours. Check to see if the pork is tender (different cuts and the amount of fat may affect the cook time). If not, cook on low for 1 more hour. If it is too runny, reduce the gravy in a saucepan. Follow step 6 in a saucepan and serve.

KERALA-STYLE BEEF CHILI

Oletherachi

SOUTH INDIA

EGG-FREE
DAIRY-FREE
GLUTEN-FREE
PEANUT-FREE
SOY-FREE

SERVES 4 ♦ PREP TIME: 20 MINUTES ♦ COOK TIME: 1 HOUR, 30 MINUTES

In the toddy shops that dot the beautiful state of Kerala, you will see men huddled over hot plates of beef chili and tall glasses of toddy (a local drink made with palm sap). They say the shops make the spiciest versions of this dish because it encourages people to drink more. You can tone the spice level to your palate, but it's worth trying out just once with at least half the quantity of spices and a couple of drinks.

- 2 tablespoons vegetable or coconut oil, divided
- 1 (2-inch) piece fresh ginger, finely chopped, divided
- 3 garlic cloves, minced
- 4 green chiles, split in half lengthwise, divided
- 2 pounds boneless beef roast, cut into small cubes
- Kosher salt
- 2 large red onions, finely chopped
- 2 tablespoons dried or fresh shredded coconut
- 1 tablespoon ground coriander
- 1 teaspoon red chili powder
- 2 teaspoons fennel seeds, roasted and ground
- 1 teaspoon turmeric powder
- 2 large tomatoes, finely chopped
- 10 curry leaves (optional)
- 3 teaspoons freshly ground black pepper
- 1 teaspoon Basic Homemade Garam Masala (page 44)

1 Heat 1 tablespoon of the oil in a large saucepan over medium heat and add the ginger, garlic, and 2 of the chiles. Sauté until fragrant, about 1 minute. Add the beef and sauté until it is slightly browned, 3 to 5 minutes.

2 Add enough water to cover the meat by 2 inches, then season with salt. Bring the liquid to a boil and simmer, uncovered, until the meat is very tender, about 45 minutes. continued ▸

3 Meanwhile, in a medium saucepan, kadhai, or wok, heat the remaining tablespoon of oil until it's shimmering. Add the onions and coconut and sauté until they are lightly browned. Turn the heat to low and add the remaining 2 chiles, coriander, chili powder, fennel, and turmeric, and sauté for about 1 minute, taking care not to burn the powders.

4 Add the tomatoes and curry leaves (if using), and sauté, mashing the tomato into the rest of the ingredients with the back of the spoon.

5 When the oil has separated slightly, add the beef with its cooking liquid, along with the black pepper. Increase the heat to high and cook uncovered, stirring occasionally, until the liquid has almost dried up, about 10 minutes. Stir in the garam masala and continue cooking until the meat is dry, 10 to 15 minutes.

6 Turn the heat to low and allow the oil to separate and coat the beef, about 5 minutes. Serve hot with fresh Easy Rice and Lentil Crêpes (page 97).

Make It Faster: Follow step 1 in the Instant Pot electric pressure cooker set on Sauté. Add the water and salt, and set the cooker to Meat Stew for approximately 7 minutes. Release the pressure using the quick method. Open to check the tenderness of the meat. If still not tender, add another 3 minutes at a time to the cooking time. When the meat is cooked to tender, remove the meat with a slotted spoon and transfer the stock to a saucepan. Reduce over medium-high heat until you have 1 cup of stock. Follow steps 3 through 6 on the stove top to finish the dish.

GOAN BEEF ROAST

WEST AND CENTRAL INDIA

DAIRY-FREE
EGG-FREE
GLUTEN-FREE
PEANUT-FREE
SOY-FREE

SERVES 2 ◆ PREP TIME: 20 MINUTES, PLUS 1 HOUR, 20 MINUTES TO OVERNIGHT TO MARINATE ◆ COOK TIME: 2 OR MORE HOURS *This recipe takes some time, but you can speed up the process in a pressure cooker or leave it in a slow cooker and go about your day. I recommend using an inexpensive cut of meat, because by the time it is done cooking, it is pull-apart tender and perfectly balanced in terms of heat and tang.*

- 1 (2-pound) beef roast
- 1 tablespoon Ginger-Garlic Paste (page 46)
- 1½ teaspoons freshly squeezed lime juice
- 2 tablespoons palm vinegar, coconut vinegar, or white vinegar
- Kosher salt
- 12 to 15 garlic cloves
- 1 (2-inch) piece fresh ginger
- 8 peppercorns
- 5 whole cloves
- 1 (3-inch) cinnamon stick
- 1 teaspoon turmeric powder
- 1 teaspoon cumin seeds
- 2 tablespoons vegetable oil
- 1½ teaspoons sugar
- 1 small red onion, thinly sliced
- 2 dried red Kashmiri chiles, broken into bits

1 Using a sharp knife, score the beef so the spices can penetrate the meat. In a large bowl, mix the beef, ginger-garlic paste, lime juice, and vinegar. Season with salt. Mix well and rub the spices and seasonings into the beef. Cover and refrigerate for at least 20 minutes.

2 In a mortar and pestle or spice grinder, mix the garlic, ginger, peppercorns, cloves, cinnamon, turmeric, and cumin seeds, and grind to a smooth paste. If the paste is too dry, add a small amount of vinegar (not water) to loosen it and make grinding easier. It should not be very runny. Add this paste to the beef and rub it into the meat with your fingers. Cover the beef again and refrigerate for at least 1 hour or overnight. continued ▶

3 In a large saucepan, heat the oil over medium heat until it's shimmering. Add the sugar and swirl the pan until the sugar caramelizes. Lift the beef out of the liquid that collected in the bowl during marinating and add it to the pan. Reserve the marinade. Brown the meat in this caramelized oil, turning at intervals, until it is nicely browned all over.

4 Add the onion, chiles, and reserved marinade to the pan. Stir the mixture and pour in about 3 cups of water, or enough to just cover the beef. Season with salt.

5 Cover the pan and cook over low heat for 2 hours, or until an instant-read thermometer inserted into the meat registers 145°F. Check the meat at 30-minute intervals to make sure the water has not dried up while cooking, and add more if needed. Serve with a side salad and Goan Fermented Steamed Buns (page 100).

Make It Faster: Follow steps 1 and 2 as written. Follow step 3 with the Instant Pot electric pressure cooker on Sauté. Then set it to Meat Stew for approximately 12 minutes. Release the pressure using the quick method and open to check the tenderness of the meat. If it is still not tender, add another 3 minutes at a time to the cooking time. When the meat is cooked to tender, transfer everything to a large saucepan. Reduce the liquid over medium-high heat until it reaches a thick consistency and coats a spoon.

Make It Easier: Follow steps 1 through 3 in a saucepan, then transfer everything to your slow cooker. Follow step 4, then cook on Low for 5 hours.

CURRY WITH BEEF MEATBALLS

ANGLO-INDIAN

DAIRY-FREE
EGG-FREE
GLUTEN-FREE
PEANUT-FREE
SOY-FREE

SERVES 4 TO 5 • PREP TIME: 30 MINUTES • COOK TIME: 40 MINUTES *This Anglo-Indian dish marries the Western concept of meatballs with Indian spices. I make it often and serve it with Aromatic Yellow Rice (page 77) or Lime Rice (page 78), or sometimes just crusty bread to soak up all the gravy.*

- 1 pound ground beef
- 1 teaspoon freshly ground black pepper
- 1½ teaspoons Basic Homemade Garam Masala (page 44), divided
- 1 green chile, finely chopped
- 1 tablespoon finely chopped cilantro leaves
- Kosher salt
- 1½ tablespoons vegetable oil
- 1 medium red onion, finely chopped
- 10 curry leaves (optional)
- 2 teaspoons Ginger-Garlic Paste (page 46)
- 2 teaspoons red chili powder
- 1 tablespoon ground coriander
- 1 teaspoon ground cumin
- ½ teaspoon turmeric powder
- 1 cup tomato purée
- 1 cup water
- ½ cup coconut milk (reserve 1 tablespoon for garnish)

1 In a large bowl, mix the ground beef, pepper, ½ teaspoon of garam masala, chile, and cilantro. Season with salt and mix well. Form the meat mixture into small balls and set them aside.

2 In a large saucepan, heat the oil over medium heat until shimmering. Turn the heat to medium-low and cook the onion and curry leaves (if using) for 5 minutes, or until the onions are transparent. Add the ginger-garlic paste and stir until fragrant, about 2 minutes.

3 Add the chili powder, coriander, cumin, and turmeric and stir for 20 seconds. Add the tomato purée and cook for 10 minutes, or until the oil separates. Add the remaining 1 teaspoon of garam masala and 1 cup of water, season with salt, and bring to a boil. Reduce the heat and simmer for 5 minutes.

4 Add the coconut milk and simmer for another 5 minutes. Drop the meatballs into the curry one at a time and cook for 7 to 10 minutes. Do not stir; simply swirl the pan to rotate the meatballs in the curry. Serve the meatballs garnished with the remaining coconut milk.

MINCED MEAT CURRY

Hyderabadi Kheema

SOUTH INDIA

EGG-FREE
GLUTEN-FREE
PEANUT-FREE
SOY-FREE

SERVES 2 ◆ PREP TIME: 20 MINUTES, PLUS 4 HOURS TO OVERNIGHT TO MARINATE ◆ COOK TIME: 45 TO 55 MINUTES *Hyderabadi meat dishes are famously cooked with a whole slew of aromatic spices and tended to for hours over slow fires or burning coals. There are many versions of Hyderabadi kheema, but this one is a personal favorite. It's rich yet delicate, and the flavors of all the individual spices seem to form a lovely symphony on your taste buds.*

8 ounces ground beef, mutton, or lamb
1 tablespoon Ginger-Garlic Paste (page 46)
1 teaspoon turmeric powder
½ cup plain yogurt
Kosher salt
4½ teaspoons ghee or vegetable oil, divided
3 to 4 whole cloves
1 (½-inch) cinnamon stick
Seeds from 2 green cardamom pods
1 teaspoon black cumin seeds, divided
½ cup finely chopped red onion
¼ cup mint leaves
1 teaspoon ground nutmeg
1 teaspoon red chili powder
3 teaspoons ground coriander
¼ cup water
½ teaspoon freshly ground black pepper
1 teaspoon Basic Homemade Garam Masala (page 44)
Lime wedges, to garnish

1 In a large bowl, using your hands or a wooden spoon, mix together the ground meat, ginger-garlic paste, turmeric, and yogurt. Season with salt. Cover and refrigerate for 15 to 20 minutes.

2 In a large skillet or kadhai over medium heat, melt 2 teaspoons of ghee (or heat 2 teaspoons of oil) over medium heat until it begins to shimmer. Add the whole cloves, cinnamon, cardamom, and ½ teaspoon of black cumin seeds. Add the chopped onion and mint leaves and cook until the onion turns golden brown.

3 Remove the skillet from the heat and transfer this mixture to a plate to cool. Grind the cooled mixture in a spice grinder or mortar and pestle, along with the nutmeg, chili powder, and coriander. Do not add water, but grind to a smooth paste.

4 Scrape this paste into the bowl with the meat and mix well. Cover the bowl and refrigerate the meat for at least 4 hours or overnight.

5 In a large saucepan or kadhai, melt the remaining 2½ teaspoons of ghee (or heat the remaining 2½ teaspoons of oil) over medium heat until it's shimmering. Add the remaining ½ teaspoon of black cumin seeds and allow them to pop slightly, about 20 seconds. Then add the meat mixture to the pan and stir well. Season with salt. Pour in ¼ cup of water, cover the pan, and cook over medium-low heat for 30 to 40 minutes, stirring occasionally and adding more water as needed so the meat doesn't dry up.

6 When the ghee has started rising to the top and the meat mixture looks well amalgamated with the spices, stir in the ground pepper and garam masala. Stir, check the seasonings, and allow the dish to cook for another 10 minutes until the meat is dry and the oil separates. Serve hot with lime wedges and Plain Basmati Rice (page 76) or any Indian flatbread.

Substitution Tip: You can make this dish vegetarian by using minced soy or minced mushrooms. In either case, do not marinate for longer than 15 minutes.

FLATTENED MINCE KEBABS

Shami Kebabs

NORTH INDIA

EGG-FREE
GLUTEN-FREE
PEANUT-FREE
SOY-FREE

MAKES ABOUT 12 KEBABS • PREP TIME: 20 MINUTES • COOK TIME: 20 MINUTES

The unique part about the cooking technique used in these delicately spiced kebabs is that the ground meat and spices are first cooked together and then ground to a fine paste. This results in a creamy, evenly spiced meat mixture that is velvety to bite into. I recommend increasing the quantities to make a little extra, to satisfy requests for second and third helpings.

2 teaspoons vegetable oil
1 black cardamom pod
1 (1-inch) cinnamon stick
3 whole cloves
1 teaspoon caraway seeds
10 peppercorns
10 ounces ground beef, goat, or lamb
½ teaspoon turmeric powder
2 tablespoons split yellow chickpeas (channa dal)
Kosher salt
½ cup water
¼ cup finely chopped red onion
2 green chiles, very finely chopped
1½ teaspoons finely chopped fresh ginger
1 tablespoon Ginger-Garlic Paste (page 46)
2 tablespoons finely chopped cilantro leaves
1 tablespoon finely chopped mint leaves
4 tablespoons ghee
Lime wedges, for garnish

1 Heat the oil in a medium saucepan over medium heat. Add the cardamom, cinnamon, cloves, caraway seeds, and peppercorns. Sauté until fragrant, about 30 seconds, then stir in the ground meat, turmeric, and chickpeas. Season with salt. Add the water, bring the mixture to a boil, and cook until the water evaporates, about 10 minutes. Remove the pan from the heat, let it cool slightly, then transfer the mixture to a food processor or blender and process until smooth and pasty.

2 Transfer the meat paste to a large bowl. Add the onion, chiles, ginger, ginger-garlic paste, cilantro, and mint, and mix well. Make your palms slightly wet so the paste doesn't stick. Using your hands, shape the meat mixture into 12 small balls and flatten the balls in your palms so that they are 2 to 3 inches in diameter and about ¾ inch thick.

3 Melt 2 tablespoons of ghee in a large skillet over medium heat until it is shimmering. Place half of the kebabs in the skillet and fry, turning occasionally, until both sides are golden brown and crisp. Transfer the cooked kebabs to a paper towel–lined plate and repeat with the remaining ghee and uncooked kebabs.

4 Serve immediately, garnished with lime wedges and Roasted Green Chile Chutney (page 116).

Cooking Tip: If you are making these kebabs in advance, I recommend lightly sautéing the onion before adding it to the mince paste so it doesn't add unnecessary moisture.

RAJASTHAN RED MEAT CURRY

Laal Maas

NORTH INDIA

EGG-FREE
GLUTEN-FREE
PEANUT-FREE
SOY-FREE

SERVES 4 ◆ PREP TIME: 20 MINUTES, PLUS 2 HOURS TO OVERNIGHT TO MARINATE ◆ COOK TIME: 1 TO 2 HOURS *Originally, laal maas was cooked by the royals on their hunting expeditions. Whatever was brought back would end up in this rich, fiery curry. Today, laal maas is made with lamb or goat. I've used Kashmiri chiles in this recipe, which are more about color than heat, but if you still think it's too spicy, you can reduce the number of chiles.*

10 to 15 dried Kashmiri chiles
1 head garlic, cloves separated and peeled
1 cup thick plain yogurt, whisked until smooth
Kosher salt
2 pounds bone-in lamb or goat roast
3 tablespoons ghee
4 Indian bay leaves or Mediterranean bay leaves
Seeds from 2 black cardamom pods
Seeds from 5 green cardamom pods
2 dried red chiles, broken into 2 to 3 pieces
1 (1-inch) cinnamon stick
1½ teaspoons cumin seeds
4 garlic cloves, sliced
1½ cups finely chopped red onions
1 tablespoon ground coriander
1 teaspoon turmeric powder
2 cups water

1 In a spice grinder or mortar and pestle, grind the dried chiles until they're finely ground, adding a little water as needed to aid in the grinding. The paste should not be too runny.

2 In a mortar and pestle, pound the garlic until it forms a paste.

3 In a large bowl, mix together the red chili paste, 3 tablespoons of garlic paste, and yogurt, and season with salt. Add the meat to the bowl and coat it thoroughly in the spice mixture. Cover and refrigerate for at least 2 hours or overnight.

4 In a large, heavy saucepan or kadhai, melt the ghee over medium heat until it begins to shimmer. Add the bay leaves, black cardamom seeds, green cardamom seeds, broken red chiles, cinnamon, and cumin seeds. Stir and sauté until fragrant, about 1 minute. Add the sliced garlic and sauté until aromatic, about 30 seconds, taking care not to burn any spices. Reduce the heat to low, add the onions, and sauté, stirring constantly, until the onions turn a nice golden brown color.

5 Add the marinade and the lamb to the pan and keep sautéing and stirring for about 10 minutes, until the oil starts separating slightly and the red color of the marinade begins to intensify.

6 Add the ground coriander and turmeric and mix well. Add 2 cups of water, season with salt, and cover the saucepan. Let the meat simmer and cook for at least 1 hour and up to 2 hours if the meat was marinated less than overnight. Check at intervals and stir to ensure that the liquid hasn't dried up. If it is getting too dry, add some water to ensure that the lamb cooks through. The lamb is done when an instant-read thermometer inserted into the meatiest part registers 145°F. Serve hot with any Indian flatbread or white rice.

Make It Faster: Follow steps 1 through 3 as written, then follow steps 4 and 5 with the Instant Pot electric pressure cooker on Sauté. Add 1 cup water instead of 2 in step 6, and set the cooker to Meat Stew for approximately 12 minutes. Release the pressure using the quick method. Open to check the tenderness of the meat. If it is still not tender, add another 3 minutes at a time to the cooking time. When the meat is tender, transfer the contents of the pot to a saucepan to cook off any remaining liquid.

Make It Easier: Follow steps 1 through 5 as written. Put everything in the slow cooker, then proceed through adding the water in step 6. Cook on Low for 6 hours.

LAMB IN GRAVY WITH POTATO STRAWS

Sali Boti

WEST AND CENTRAL INDIA

EGG-FREE
DAIRY-FREE
GLUTEN-FREE
PEANUT-FREE
SOY-FREE

SERVES 2 • PREP TIME: 15 MINUTES • COOK TIME: 1 HOUR, 5 MINUTES *This is another favorite from the Parsi community in Mumbai and Gujarat. Tender chunks of lamb or mutton cooked in a tangy, sweet, and hot gravy are garnished with crisp straw potatoes to give you the most delicious range of flavors and textures. I always keep some extra potatoes on the side so guests can add more to their plates.*

- 2 pounds boneless lamb roast, cubed
- 2 tablespoons Ginger-Garlic Paste (page 46), divided
- Kosher salt
- 2 tablespoons vegetable oil
- 1 cup finely chopped red onion
- ½ cup tomato purée
- 1 green chile, finely chopped
- 1 teaspoon turmeric powder
- 3 to 4 teaspoons red chili powder
- 2 teaspoons ground cumin
- 1 teaspoon Coriander-Cumin Spice Blend (page 43)
- 1 teaspoon Basic Homemade Garam Masala (page 44)
- 1 tablespoon palm vinegar, coconut vinegar, or white vinegar
- 1 tablespoon grated jaggery or 1½ teaspoons sugar
- 1½ cups water
- ½ cup straw potatoes (sali) or shoestring potatoes or crushed potato chips

1 In a large bowl, mix the lamb cubes with 1 tablespoon of the ginger-garlic paste. Season with salt. Cover and refrigerate.

2 Heat the oil in a large saucepan over medium heat until it begins to shimmer. Add the onion and sauté, stirring constantly, until it turns golden brown. Reduce the heat to medium-low, add the remaining 1 tablespoon of ginger-garlic paste, and stir until fragrant, about 30 seconds, taking care not to burn the onion or the paste. Add a few drops of water if the browning is too quick.

3 Add the tomato purée and sauté until the oil separates from the onion and tomato mixture. Add the chile, turmeric, chili powder, cumin, coriander-cumin blend, and garam masala, and cook, stirring constantly, for 30 seconds.

4 Add the marinated lamb and stir to coat with the spiced oil for 1 or 2 minutes. Add the vinegar, jaggery, and 1½ cups of water. Cover the pan and cook the lamb over low heat for 1 hour, until the liquid has reduced by half. Check at intervals and stir to ensure that the liquid hasn't dried up. If it is getting too dry, add some more water.

5 When the meat is very tender, check the seasonings and adjust the vinegar, sugar, and salt as desired; it should be tangy, spicy, and slightly sweet. Serve the lamb and sauce in bowls garnished with crisp straw potatoes or crushed potato chips.

Make It Faster: Follow step 1 as written. Follow steps 2 and 3 with the Instant Pot electric pressure cooker on Sauté. In step 4, set the cooker to Meat Stew for approximately 10 minutes. Release the pressure using the quick method. Open to check the tenderness of the meat. If still not tender, add another 3 minutes at a time to the cooking time. When the meat is tender, transfer the contents of the pot to a saucepan to cook off any excess liquid.

9

EGGS, FISH, AND SEAFOOD

SPICED SCRAMBLED EGGS

Anda Bhurji

ALL INDIA

VEGETARIAN
GLUTEN-FREE
PEANUT-FREE
SOY-FREE

SERVES 2 ◆ PREP TIME: 15 MINUTES ◆ COOK TIME: 10 MINUTES *The humble scrambled egg gets a makeover in the Indian kitchen. In some homes, the bhurji is so loved that it is served as a side dish at lunch or dinner. When you know this basic bhurji recipe, you can get as creative as you like with curry leaves, cumin seeds, and more.*

2 tablespoons vegetable oil
1 medium red onion, finely chopped
2 medium tomatoes, finely chopped
3 green chiles, split in half lengthwise
2 teaspoons Ginger-Garlic Paste (optional) (page 46)
1 teaspoon red chili powder
½ teaspoon turmeric powder
½ teaspoon ground coriander (optional)
4 eggs, lightly whisked
Kosher salt
2 teaspoons unsalted butter, divided
¼ cup chopped cilantro leaves, divided

1 In a medium skillet, heat the oil over medium heat until it's shimmering. Add the onion and sauté until softened, about 1 minute. If the onion starts to brown, turn the heat down or add a few drops of water.

2 Add the tomatoes and sauté until soft, mashing them with the back of the spoon, about 1 minute. Add the chiles and ginger-garlic paste (if using), stirring until fragrant. Add the chili powder, turmeric, and coriander (if using), stirring for 30 seconds, just until the oil separates from the paste.

3 Reduce the heat to low. Add the whisked eggs and season with salt. Gently stir for 1 minute or until the mixture curdles. Increase the heat to medium. Vigorously stir the egg mixture and break up the bigger clumps. Add 1 teaspoon of butter as you stir and let it melt into the egg mixture.

4 Add half of the chopped cilantro and mix it in for about 30 seconds. Turn the heat off and serve immediately with the rest of the cilantro as garnish and a teaspoon of butter dolloped on top. Serve with bread.

Serving Tip: You can serve this scrambled egg dish with Deep-Fried Bread (page 96).

INDIAN SPICED OMELET

Masala Omelet

ALL INDIA

VEGETARIAN
DAIRY-FREE
GLUTEN-FREE
PEANUT-FREE
SOY-FREE

SERVES 2 ◆ PREP TIME: 10 MINUTES ◆ COOK TIME: 5 MINUTES *Onion, chiles, and fresh herbs make the masala omelet a different and delicious take on the fluffed-up Western version. It's a quick, tasty breakfast, and in some parts of India, a popular anytime street snack, filled with cheese and sprinkles of chaat masala. I like to have mine with some Indian pav, a white-bread bun that's popular in West India.*

4 eggs
Kosher salt
2 tablespoons finely chopped red onion
1 to 2 green chiles, chopped
1 tablespoon finely chopped tomato
¼ teaspoon turmeric powder
¼ teaspoon red chili powder (optional)
1 tablespoon chopped cilantro leaves and tender stems
3 tablespoons vegetable oil, divided

1 In a medium bowl, season the eggs with salt, and beat them until they're lightly frothy. Add the onion, chiles, tomato, turmeric, chili powder (if using), and cilantro; whisk to mix.

2 In a medium cast-iron skillet, heat 1½ tablespoons of oil over medium heat until it's shimmering. Stir the egg mixture again, so that the vegetables are dispersed throughout. Pour half the egg mixture into the hot pan. Cook until the underside is lightly browned and set, about 1 minute. Flip the omelet and cook the other side for another minute. Remove the omelet from the pan and repeat the process with the remaining oil and egg mixture. Serve hot with bread or toast and Masala Chai (page 227).

Serving Tip: To make this dish even heartier, fill the omelets with grated cheese or serve them with tomato sauce and Roasted Green Chile Chutney (page 116) as a dip on the side.

EGG, POTATO, AND CHUTNEY BALLS

Chutney Eeda Pattice

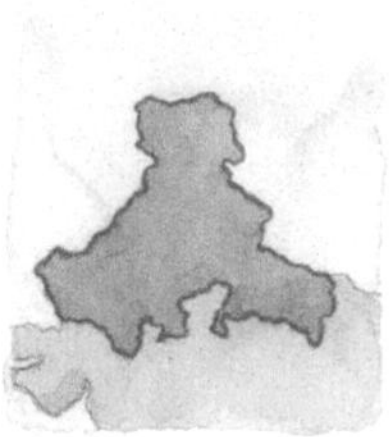

NORTH INDIA

VEGETARIAN
DAIRY-FREE
GLUTEN-FREE
PEANUT-FREE
SOY-FREE
ALLIUM-FREE

MAKES 12 BALLS • PREP TIME: 15 MINUTES • COOK TIME: 20 MINUTES

This variation on the Scotch egg uses potatoes instead of meat. It's a lovely dish to serve when entertaining, as it looks quite impressive once you cut it open to reveal the green of the cilantro chutney and the yellow and white of the egg. This dish is another popular one in the Indian Parsi community in Maharashtra.

- 4 medium potatoes, boiled, mashed, and cooled
- Leaves from 1 small bunch cilantro
- 1½ tablespoons fresh, or frozen and thawed, grated coconut
- 1 teaspoon cumin seeds
- 2 to 3 green chiles
- 6 garlic cloves
- Kosher salt
- ½ teaspoon sugar
- 3 hardboiled eggs, cut lengthwise into quarters
- 4 tablespoons vegetable oil
- 1 egg, beaten

1 Using a tablespoon, scoop up 12 balls of mashed potato. You should have some left over. In your hands, knead each ball until it is smooth, and create an indentation on the top of each to form a cup.

2 In a mortar and pestle, blender, or spice grinder, process the cilantro, coconut, cumin, chiles, garlic, salt, and sugar. Place a teaspoon of this paste into the well in the center of each potato ball. You will have some of this chutney left over.

3 Place an egg quarter in each chutney-filled hollow. Cover with more mashed potatoes until the egg and chutney are sealed inside. Try to shape the balls into oblongs, like eggs.

4 In a large nonstick or cast-iron skillet, heat the oil over medium-high heat until it's shimmering. Dip each ball in the beaten egg and gently place it in the oil. Fry, turning frequently, until the ball is golden on each side, 5 to 7 minutes total. Transfer the cooked potato ball to a paper towel–lined plate and repeat with the remaining balls. Serve hot with the remaining chutney.

BENGALI EGG CURRY

Egg Kalia

EAST INDIA

VEGETARIAN
DAIRY-FREE
GLUTEN-FREE
PEANUT-FREE
SOY-FREE

SERVES 2 ◆ PREP TIME: 15 MINUTES ◆ COOK TIME: 20 MINUTES *A kalia is a rich gravy in Bengali cuisine, and egg kalia is one of the most popular dishes from the state of West Bengal. The hardboiled eggs are cooked in oil until they are crunchy and golden brown. The whole spices make it quite an aromatic dish, and the touch of sugar adds a nice balance.*

2 hardboiled eggs, peeled
1½ teaspoons turmeric powder, divided
2 tablespoons vegetable oil
Seeds from 2 cardamom pods
2 whole cloves
1 (1-inch) cinnamon stick
2 medium red onions, chopped
1½ teaspoons sugar
1 tablespoon Ginger-Garlic Paste (page 46)
2 green chiles, chopped
1 medium tomato, chopped
2 teaspoons red chili powder
½ cup plus 2 teaspoons water, divided
Kosher salt
1½ teaspoons melted ghee or vegetable oil (optional)
2 teaspoons Basic Homemade Garam Masala (page 44)
Fresh cilantro leaves, for garnishing

1 Coat the hardboiled eggs with ½ teaspoon of the turmeric.

2 In a medium saucepan, kadhai, or wok, heat the oil over medium-high heat until it's shimmering. Add the eggs and sauté until golden brown on all sides, 3 to 5 minutes. Using a slotted spoon, transfer the eggs to a plate.

3 To the same oil, add the cardamom, cloves, and cinnamon and sauté until fragrant. Add the onions and sugar and sauté until the onions are golden brown. continued ▶

4 Stir in the ginger-garlic paste and chiles. Add the chopped tomato, the remaining 1 teaspoon of turmeric, the chili powder, and 2 teaspoons of water. Stir well and cook until the tomatoes soften and the oil separates.

5 Add ½ cup of water, season with salt, and return the eggs to the pan. Cook for 8 minutes, or until the sauce thickens slightly. Sprinkle the ghee (if using) and garam masala over the curry; mix well. Serve hot, garnished with cilantro leaves, alongside any rice or Indian bread.

Substitution Tip: You can make this vegan by using cubed tofu or winter squash instead of eggs.

TANGY ASSAMESE FISH CURRY

Masor Tenga

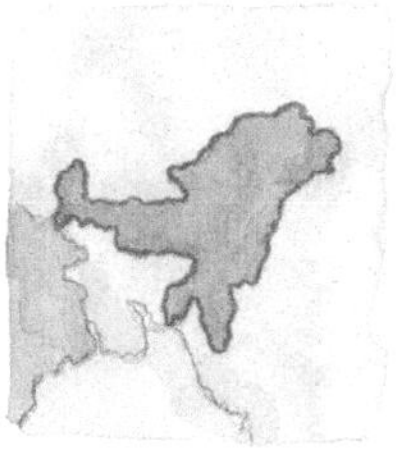

NORTHEAST INDIA

EGG-FREE
DAIRY-FREE
GLUTEN-FREE
PEANUT-FREE
SOY-FREE
ALLIUM-FREE

SERVES 4 ◆ PREP TIME: 10 MINUTES, PLUS 10 MINUTES TO MARINATE ◆ COOK TIME: 30 MINUTES *East and Northeast India are well known for their river fish dishes. This one from Assam is a tangy, light curry that uses rohu, a kind of carp, along with tomatoes, lemon, and a few mild spices that lend the dish a refreshing twist.*

8 (½-inch-thick) fillets of carp or other freshwater, white-fleshed fish
1 teaspoon turmeric powder, divided
Kosher salt
3 tablespoons vegetable oil, divided
½ teaspoon fenugreek seeds
2 green chiles, stemmed and split in half lengthwise
4 ripe tomatoes, chopped
1½ cups warm water
1 to 2 teaspoons freshly squeezed lemon juice
3 tablespoons chopped cilantro leaves

1 In an airtight container, sprinkle the fish with ½ teaspoon of turmeric and season with salt. Cover and refrigerate for at least 10 minutes.

2 In a large skillet, heat 1½ tablespoons of oil over medium heat until shimmering. Fry the fish until lightly browned and just cooked, about 5 minutes, working in batches. Transfer the cooked fish to a paper towel–lined plate.

3 Heat the remaining 1½ tablespoons of oil in a medium saucepan over medium heat until shimmering. Add the fenugreek seeds. When they turn light brown, transfer them to a small bowl. Set aside. continued ▶

4 To the same oil over medium-low heat, add the chiles and tomatoes. Mash the tomatoes with the back of the spoon as they cook, and continue cooking until they release their liquid and the oil begins to separate, 5 to 7 minutes. Season with salt and the remaining ½ teaspoon turmeric. Stir well.

5 Slide the fried fish pieces into the pan. Add the warm water and simmer for 10 minutes. Reduce the heat to low, add the lemon juice, and remove the pan from the heat. Stir in the chopped cilantro and garnish with the fenugreek seeds. Serve hot with steamed rice.

Ingredient Tip: If you find that the tomatoes sold in your area are sweeter rather than tangier, increase the lemon juice by another couple of teaspoons.

FISH IN FRAGRANT COCONUT MILK CURRY

Meen Moilee

SOUTH INDIA

EGG-FREE
DAIRY-FREE
GLUTEN-FREE
PEANUT-FREE
SOY-FREE

SERVES 2 ◆ PREP TIME: 15 MINUTES ◆ COOK TIME: 20 MINUTES *This is a very mild dish that enhances the flavor of the fish, so it is important to use fresh, firm white-fleshed fish in this recipe. It is a personal favorite of mine because it is so unlike the other fish curries of India, which use red chiles. The color of this dish is half its charm—a bright, inviting yellow.*

4 fillets of any firm white-fleshed ocean fish, such as pomfret, barramundi, or kingfish
1½ teaspoon turmeric powder, divided
Kosher salt
1½ tablespoons coconut or vegetable oil
2 whole cloves
Seeds from 1 green cardamom pod
1 (½-inch) cinnamon stick
1 tablespoon grated fresh ginger
1½ teaspoons grated garlic
1 medium red onion, thinly sliced
3 green chiles, split in half lengthwise
10 to 12 curry leaves (optional)
1 cup thin coconut milk (½ cup coconut milk diluted with ½ cup water)
1 large tomato, chopped
½ cup full-fat coconut milk

1 In a large bowl, marinate the fish with ½ teaspoon of turmeric. Season with salt, cover, and refrigerate for at least 10 minutes.

2 In a saucepan, kadhai, or wok, heat the oil over medium heat until it's shimmering. Add the cloves, cardamom, and cinnamon and stir until fragrant, about 1 minute. Add the ginger, garlic, onion, and chiles and stir until the mixture is fragrant and the onion softens, about 5 minutes.

3 Add the curry leaves (if using), and stand back as they crackle. Stir until fragrant, about 30 seconds. Add the remaining 1 teaspoon of turmeric to the oil, stir briskly, and immediately add the thin coconut milk. Season with salt. Add the tomato and allow the curry to come to a gentle boil, uncovered.

4 Turn the heat to low, add the marinated fish, and cook until it is opaque and easily flaked with a fork, 8 to 10 minutes. Add the full-fat coconut milk and bring the curry to a gentle boil for about 1 minute. Serve hot with Plain Basmati Rice (page 76) or Easy Rice and Lentil Crêpes (page 97).

FISH STEAMED IN BANANA LEAVES

Patra ni Macchi

WEST AND CENTRAL INDIA

DAIRY-FREE
EGG-FREE
GLUTEN-FREE
PEANUT-FREE
SOY-FREE

SERVES 4 ◆ PREP TIME: 15 MINUTES ◆ COOK TIME: 20 TO 30 MINUTES

This simple steamed fish dish from Maharashtra is eagerly anticipated at Parsi weddings, but it's so easy to make that you can whip it up on even the busiest weeknight. The coconut- and chile-flavored fish is fragrant and comforting, and is steamed in banana leaves for a striking presentation. If you can't find banana leaves, you can always use aluminum foil.

- 1 teaspoon kosher salt
- ½ teaspoon turmeric powder
- 2 medium butterfish (or other whole white fish), sliced in half through the backbone, gutted, heads removed
- 1 cup fresh, or frozen and thawed, grated coconut
- 3 tablespoons coarsely chopped cilantro leaves and stems
- 5 to 8 green chiles
- 1 tablespoon cumin seeds
- 7 to 10 garlic cloves
- 1½ tablespoons sugar
- 1 teaspoon vegetable oil
- 2 tablespoons freshly squeezed lemon juice
- 4 pieces banana leaf or aluminum foil, cut to about double the size of the fish pieces
- 4 pieces kitchen twine

1 In an airtight container large enough to fit both fish, mix the salt and turmeric. Rub the spice mixture into the fish; cover and refrigerate for at least 10 minutes.

2 In a mortar and pestle, blender, or spice grinder, blend the coconut, cilantro, chiles, cumin, garlic, sugar, oil, and lemon juice. Spread this paste all over the butterfish and place each fish in the center of a piece of banana leaf/aluminum foil. Wrap tightly on all sides, as you would a parcel, and secure with kitchen twine.

3 Place the fish parcels in a bamboo steamer or raised steaming stand and set the steamer in a large saucepan filled with 2 inches of water. Bring the water to a simmer over medium heat and steam the fish for 20 to 30 minutes, depending on the thickness of the pieces. When it's done, the fish should be easily flaked with a fork. Serve hot.

Substitution Tip: Butterfish is commonly found at Indian or Asian markets. If you can't get your hands on it, you can use any other delicate, nonoily, white fish, such as tilapia or catfish.

Ingredient Tip: If you are having trouble with stiff leaves, graze the leaf over the stove top's open flame for just a few seconds or buzz it in the microwave for 15 seconds.

SPICED FRIED FISH

Chepa Vepudu

SOUTH INDIA

EGG-FREE
DAIRY-FREE
GLUTEN-FREE
PEANUT-FREE
SOY-FREE

SERVES 2 ◆ PREP TIME: 10 MINUTES, PLUS 20 MINUTES TO MARINATE ◆ COOK TIME: 10 MINUTES *Fried fish in India is prepared in ways that reflect the spices that are grown in that region. The spices are traditionally thought to remove the fishy aroma and add taste to the delicate flesh. This recipe from Andhra Pradesh also uses curry leaves as a garnish to give this dish a distinctly South Indian flavor.*

1 teaspoon turmeric powder
2 teaspoons red chili powder
½ teaspoon ground cumin
¼ teaspoon freshly ground black pepper (optional)
½ teaspoon ground coriander
Juice of 1 large lime (about 1½ tablespoons)
1 tablespoon Ginger-Garlic Paste (page 46)
4 kingfish fillets (or mackerel or tilapia fillets)
Kosher salt
2 tablespoons vegetable oil
10 curry leaves (optional)
Lime wedges, for garnish

1 In a large bowl, mix the turmeric, chili powder, cumin, pepper (if using), coriander, lime juice, and ginger-garlic paste. Apply this evenly on the fish fillets and season them with salt. Cover and refrigerate for at least 20 minutes.

2 In a frying pan, heat the oil over medium heat until it's shimmering. Add the curry leaves (if using), and let them crackle. Remove the curry leaves and set aside. In the same oil, add the marinated fish and cook for 3 to 4 minutes, turning to cook on both sides, until the fish is cooked.

3 Drain and serve with the curry leaves sprinkled on top and lime wedges as a garnish. Serve with rice and dal, or Easy Rice and Lentil Crêpes (page 97) or roti.

Cooking Tip: For a crispier crust, coat the fish in semolina before frying. This is known as rava fried fish, and is common in most parts of West and South India.

Substitution Tip: Instead of lime in the marinade, you can use the same amount of tamarind extract or white vinegar.

MANCHURIAN FISH

INDIAN-CHINESE

EGG-FREE
DAIRY-FREE
GLUTEN-FREE
PEANUT-FREE

SERVES 2 ◆ PREP TIME: 20 MINUTES ◆ COOK TIME: 10 MINUTES *Indian-Chinese food is more Indian than Chinese and has evolved to blend bold Indian spices with Chinese cooking techniques. This is my version of Manchurian fish, which you'll find in every Chinese restaurant in India. I leave out the battering and deep frying, since I prefer the taste of the fish coming through in the sauce.*

- 1 teaspoon Ginger-Garlic Paste (page 46)
- 3 teaspoons palm vinegar, coconut vinegar, or white vinegar, divided
- 1 teaspoon freshly ground black pepper, divided
- 1¼ teaspoons red chili powder, divided
- 1 pound boneless, cubed white fish such as tilapia or pomfret
- Kosher salt
- 1½ tablespoons vegetable oil
- 4 garlic cloves, finely chopped
- 1 (1-inch) piece fresh ginger, finely chopped
- 2 green chiles, finely chopped
- 3 scallions, white parts only, finely chopped (chop and save the green pieces for garnish)
- 2 tablespoons soy sauce
- 1 tablespoon tomato sauce
- 1 tablespoon Szechuan Chutney (page 117)
- Sugar
- ¼ cup plus 3 tablespoons water, divided
- 3 teaspoons cornstarch

1 In a large bowl, mix together the ginger-garlic paste, 1 teaspoon of vinegar, ½ teaspoon of pepper, and ¼ teaspoon of chili powder. Add the fish and rub the mixture into its flesh. Season with salt. Cover and refrigerate for at least 10 minutes.

2 Heat the oil in a frying pan, wok, or kadhai over medium heat until it begins to shimmer. Add the chopped garlic, ginger, and chiles and stir until fragrant, about 1 minute. Add the white parts of the scallion and sauté for 30 seconds. Add the remaining teaspoon of chili powder, the soy sauce, the remaining ½ teaspoon of pepper, the tomato sauce, the Szechuan chutney, and the remaining 2 teaspoons of vinegar. Reduce the heat to medium-low and cook for about 2 minutes. Taste the sauce to check for seasoning, and add salt or sugar as needed. It should have a slightly sweet taste for balance. continued ▶

3 Add the fish and pour in ¼ cup of water. Let the fish cook until it is flaky and opaque, 2 to 3 minutes.

4 In a small bowl, mix the cornstarch with 3 tablespoons of water and stir until no lumps remain. Add this mixture to the fish and cook until the sauce starts to thicken, 3 to 4 minutes. Stir very carefully to prevent the fish from breaking too much. Garnish with the reserved scallion greens and serve with Szechuan Fried Basmati Rice (page 82).

Substitution Tip: You can follow the same recipe and use shrimp or squid rings or even crabmeat balls instead of the fish.

GOAN SHRIMP AND OKRA CURRY

Sungta ani Bende Kodi

WEST AND CENTRAL INDIA

EGG-FREE
DAIRY-FREE
GLUTEN-FREE
PEANUT-FREE
SOY-FREE

SERVES 2 ◆ PREP TIME: 15 MINUTES ◆ COOK TIME: 25 MINUTES *This shrimp curry is a Goan staple, cooked almost every week in homes across the state when seafood is plentiful. Most West India seafood curries like this one have a bold souring agent added, as it is believed to cut the fishiness, aid digestion, and mellow the heat of the chiles.*

- 1 cup tightly packed fresh, or frozen and thawed, grated coconut
- 8 to 10 dried red Kashmiri chiles
- ½ teaspoon turmeric powder
- 2 tablespoons coriander seeds
- 1 teaspoon cumin seeds
- 10 to 12 peppercorns
- 3 garlic cloves
- 2 tablespoons vegetable or coconut oil
- 1 medium red onion, chopped
- 1 tomato, chopped
- 10 ounces shrimp, peeled and deveined
- 3 dried kokum pods or 2 tablespoons slivered raw green mango (optional)
- 1 cup water
- Kosher salt
- Pinch sugar (optional)
- 10 medium okra pods
- 1½ teaspoons tamarind flesh soaked in a little warm water or 1 tablespoon tamarind paste diluted in 1 tablespoon water

1 In a mortar and pestle or spice grinder, grind the coconut, Kashmiri chiles, turmeric, coriander seeds, cumin seeds, peppercorns, and garlic cloves to create a fine paste.

2 In a saucepan, wok, or kadhai, heat the oil over medium heat until it's shimmering. Add the onion and sauté until it turns translucent and soft. Add the tomato and cook until it softens. continued ▶

3 Add the paste from step 1 and sauté, stirring constantly, for 5 to 8 minutes. Add the shrimp and kokum (if using) and stir well. Add the water, season with salt, and add the sugar (if using).

4 Bring the curry to a simmer. Add the okra and tamarind, bring the curry to a rolling boil, and cook, uncovered, until the okra is tender, about 10 minutes. Remove the pan from the heat. Serve hot with Plain Basmati Rice (page 76).

Ingredient Tip: Kokum is a fruit that grows abundantly on the western coast of India. It is sun-dried and used throughout the year as a souring agent in the region's cuisine. Try to get these dried plums at an Indian grocery store. They will keep for 1 year stored in an airtight container in the refrigerator.

GOAN PRAWN AND COCONUT CURRY

WEST AND CENTRAL INDIA

EGG-FREE
DAIRY-FREE
GLUTEN-FREE
PEANUT-FREE
SOY-FREE

SERVES 2 ♦ PREP TIME: 15 MINUTES ♦ COOK TIME: 20 MINUTES *Two things that are available abundantly in Goa on the western shores of India are coconut and seafood. This dish represents that abundance. It's delicate, balanced, and delicious served on a bed of white rice.*

- ½ cup tightly packed fresh, or frozen and thawed, grated coconut
- 8 dried red Kashmiri chiles
- ½ teaspoon turmeric powder
- 2 tablespoons coriander seeds
- 1 teaspoon cumin seeds
- 10 to 12 peppercorns
- 3 garlic cloves
- 2 tablespoons vegetable or coconut oil
- 1 medium red onion, chopped
- 10 ounces shrimp, peeled and deveined
- 1 cup water
- Kosher salt
- Pinch sugar (optional)
- 1 tablespoon tamarind extract, diluted in 1 tablespoon water
- 5 to 6 curry leaves, for garnish (optional)
- Lime wedges, for garnish (optional)

1 In a mortar and pestle or spice grinder, grind the coconut, Kashmiri chiles, turmeric, coriander seeds, cumin seeds, peppercorns, and garlic cloves to create a fine paste.

2 In a saucepan, wok, or kadhai, heat the oil over medium heat until it's shimmering. Add the onion and sauté until it turns translucent and soft. Add the masala paste and sauté, stirring constantly, for 5 to 8 minutes.

3 Add the shrimp and stir well. Add the water, season with salt, and add the sugar (if using). Bring the curry to a simmer.

4 Stir in the diluted tamarind extract and let the curry come to a rolling boil. Turn off the heat and serve with Plain Basmati Rice (page 76). Garnish with torn curry leaves and lime wedges on the side, if you like.

Substitution Tip: If you cannot find fresh or frozen grated coconut, use 1 cup coconut milk instead. Grind the ingredients in step 1 and add the coconut milk in step 2, after sautéing the spice paste.

SHRIMP IN COCONUT CREAM SAUCE

Chingri Malai Kari

EAST INDIA

FESTIVAL FOOD

EGG-FREE
DAIRY-FREE
GLUTEN-FREE
PEANUT-FREE
SOY-FREE

SERVES 4 ◆ PREP TIME: 15 MINUTES, PLUS 30 MINUTES TO MARINATE ◆ COOK TIME: 20 MINUTES *Chingri malai kari uses shrimp or baby lobster, and almost every Bengali family I know has their own special recipe for it. It is a favorite dish at Bengali festivals such as their New Year's, and this recipe is my favorite version. I like to serve it in a hollowed-out green coconut when I'm entertaining, for a rustic touch.*

- 1 pound medium shrimp, shelled and deveined, or head kept on and deveined
- 1½ teaspoons turmeric powder, divided
- Kosher salt
- 2 medium red onions, chopped
- 2 tablespoons vegetable oil
- 1 (1-inch) cinnamon stick
- 3 green cardamom pods
- 2 whole cloves
- 2 Indian bay leaves or Mediterranean bay leaves
- 3 garlic cloves, cut in slivers
- 2 teaspoons finely chopped ginger
- 1 teaspoon sugar
- ½ teaspoon red chili powder
- 1 teaspoon ground cumin
- 2 cups coconut milk
- ½ cup water
- 2 green chiles, split in half lengthwise

1 In a small bowl, toss together the shrimp and ½ teaspoon turmeric. Season with salt. Cover and refrigerate for at least 30 minutes.

2 In a blender, process the onions to create a thick paste.

3 Heat the oil in a medium skillet over medium heat until shimmering. Add the shrimp and cook until barely opaque, 2 to 3 minutes. Using a slotted spoon, transfer the shrimp to a plate.

4 To the same oil, add the cinnamon, cardamom, cloves, and bay leaves; fry until fragrant. Add the garlic and ginger and cook for about 20 seconds, then add the onion paste and sugar and cook until most of the moisture evaporates and the onions turn golden brown, about 5 minutes.

5 Add the chili powder, cumin, and the remaining teaspoon of turmeric. Season with salt, then stir in the coconut milk and water.

6 Bring to a boil, uncovered. Reduce the heat to low, add the chiles and shrimp, and cook for another 5 to 7 minutes, until the oil starts floating on the top of the curry and it looks creamy. Serve hot with white rice.

Ingredient Tip: Keeping the heads of the shrimp on adds more flavor. You can just snap them off as you eat.

Cooking Tip: Do not cover the pan when you are cooking this curry, as this may cause the coconut milk to split or curdle.

SPICY SQUID STIR-FRY

Kanava Roast

SOUTH INDIA

VEGAN
GLUTEN-FREE
PEANUT-FREE
SOY-FREE

SERVES 2 TO 3 • PREP TIME: 20 MINUTES • COOK TIME: 15 MINUTES *Kerala is famous for its fiery, spice-laden food. This squid stir-fry or roast (a name given to this type of dry style of preparation in this region) is laced with pepper, fennel, and garam masala. Though it is hot, you can eat small quantities of it with white rice or Easy Rice and Lentil Crêpes (page 97) to help cut the spice.*

1 pound squid, cleaned and cut into rings
1 teaspoon turmeric powder, divided
Kosher salt
10 shallots or 2 large red onions, chopped
2 green chiles, chopped
1 (1-inch) piece fresh ginger, chopped
6 garlic cloves, chopped
1½ tablespoons coconut or vegetable oil
25 curry leaves (optional), divided
1 medium tomato, chopped
1½ teaspoons red Kashmiri chili powder
½ teaspoon ground coriander
1 teaspoon freshly ground black pepper
½ teaspoon Basic Homemade Garam Masala (page 44)
½ teaspoon ground fennel seeds

1 In a medium bowl, toss together the squid and ½ teaspoon of turmeric. Season with salt and set aside.

2 In a mortar and pestle, blender, or spice grinder, process the shallots, chiles, ginger, and garlic into a thick paste.

3 In a medium saucepan, wok, or kadhai, heat the oil over medium-high heat until it shimmers. Add 15 curry leaves (if using) and the masala paste to the pan. Sauté for 1 minute, then add the tomato and cook until it softens and the oil separates, about 5 minutes. If it starts to stick, add a few drops of water.

4 Reduce the heat to low and add the chili powder, the coriander, the remaining ½ teaspoon turmeric, and the pepper. Stir briskly for 1 minute, then add the squid and cook for 7 to 8 minutes, or longer if the rings are thicker. Check the seasoning and add more salt or other seasonings as desired.

5 Add the garam masala and ground fennel and cook for a few more minutes, until the masala is thick and coats the squid rings. Garnish with the remaining 10 curry leaves (if using) and serve warm.

Substitution Tip: Instead of squid, you can use shrimp or even chopped hard-boiled egg.

CLAMS IN DRY-SPICED COCONUT PASTE

Kube Sukhe

SOUTH INDIA

EGG-FREE
DAIRY-FREE
GLUTEN-FREE
PEANUT-FREE
SOY-FREE

SERVES 2 ◆ PREP TIME: 15 MINUTES, PLUS 20 MINUTES TO SOAK ◆ COOK TIME: 25 MINUTES *Indian fish markets are such a delight: bright colors, feisty fisherwomen, and seemingly endless haggling over fish until both buyer and seller are pleased. Clams are usually an inexpensive choice and are brought home alive, snapping their shells away. This recipe, from the southern state of Karnataka, uses this bountiful shellfish alongside coconut and a host of simple spices.*

¾ pound clams
Kosher salt
5 dried red chiles or 2 teaspoons red chili powder
1 teaspoon turmeric powder
5 peppercorns
1 medium red onion, chopped
1 teaspoon tamarind pulp
1 tablespoon vegetable oil
5 garlic cloves, crushed
1 teaspoon black mustard seeds
¾ cup fresh, or frozen and thawed, grated coconut

1 Place the clams in a large bowl and cover them with cold water. Set them aside to soak for 20 minutes.

2 When the clams have finished soaking, transfer them to a medium saucepan, pour in enough cold water to cover them by 1 inch, and season the water generously with salt. Bring the water to a boil, cover the pan, and simmer for about 10 minutes, or until the clams open. Turn off the heat and do not stir.

3 Using a slotted spoon, transfer the clams to a clean bowl, leaving the stock behind in the saucepan for the sediment to settle. Discard any clams that have not opened.

4 Remove and discard the empty shell from each clam, retaining the flesh still attached to the other side. Check the shells with the retained flesh for any sand or sediment, and clean under running water if necessary.

5 In a mortar and pestle, blender, or spice grinder, process the chiles, turmeric, peppercorns, onion, and tamarind until they form a smooth paste.

6 In a saucepan, wok, or kadhai, heat the oil over medium heat until it's shimmering. Sauté the garlic until lightly browned. Add the mustard seeds and let them crackle. Turn the heat to low and then add the ground masala paste. Keep stirring and cooking until fragrant, 5 to 7 minutes. If the spices begin to burn or stick to the bottom of the pan, add a little water or reserved stock.

7 Add the clams and coconut to the saucepan. Mix to coat the clams in the thick paste and cook until the masala paste and the clams are well mixed, about 5 minutes. Season with salt. Serve hot with Plain Basmati Rice (page 76) or Easy Rice and Lentil Crêpes (page 97).

Cooking Tip: Don't stir the clams or the stock left behind if you plan to use some of it in the cooking process. Allow any sediments to settle to the bottom before using only the surface stock.

10

DRINKS AND DESSERTS

PUNJABI LASSI

NORTH INDIA

VEGETARIAN
EGG-FREE
GLUTEN-FREE
PEANUT-FREE
SOY-FREE
ALLIUM-FREE

SERVES 2 ◆ PREP TIME: 10 MINUTES *You haven't experienced indulgence until you've had a lassi in Punjab—freshly made thick yogurt churned with sugar, cardamom, and full-fat milk and garnished with white butter (called "makhan") in the glass. If you can't get Indian white butter, a good substitute is heavy cream.*

10 small yellow cardamom pods
2 cups chilled thick plain yogurt
5 tablespoons sugar
2 teaspoons rose water (optional)
1½ to 2 cups chilled water or milk
2 to 3 strands of saffron, plus more for garnish (optional)
6 ice cubes (optional)
1 tablespoon heavy cream or Indian white butter
2 tablespoons slivered nuts, such as almonds or pistachios, for garnish

1 Remove the seeds from the cardamom pods and grind them to a fine powder in a mortar and pestle or spice grinder.

2 Place the yogurt in a large mixing bowl. Using a whisk or an electric beater on low speed, beat the yogurt until it is completely smooth. Add the cardamom and sugar and blend well.

3 Add the rose water (if using) and the chilled water or milk (more or less, depending on how thick you like your lassi), and keep beating until the consistency is smooth and a frothy layer forms on top. Stir in the saffron strands (if using).

4 Put the ice cubes (if using) in tall serving glasses and pour the lassi over the ice. Garnish with the heavy cream or white butter, slivered nuts, and a few more saffron strands.

Make It Healthier: You can reduce the fat content by using low-fat or fat-free yogurt and omitting the cream or butter garnish.

Cooking Tip: Think of this as a basic lassi recipe, to which you can add fruits like mango and strawberry, some grated nutmeg, or whatever else you'd like.

MINT LASSI

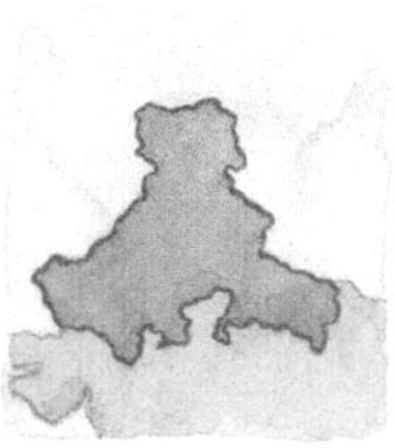

NORTH INDIA

VEGETARIAN
GLUTEN-FREE
EGG-FREE
PEANUT-FREE
SOY-FREE
ALLIUM-FREE

SERVES 2 ◆ PREP TIME: 10 MINUTES *This variation on the classic lassi is cooling and refreshing with its use of mint. You could also add fruits that go well with mint, such as mango, to make it even more interesting. Or go the savory route by making a salted lassi with cumin powder (see the Cooking Tip below).*

- Seeds from 5 small yellow cardamom pods
- 2 tablespoons mint leaves, plus leaves for garnish
- 2 cups chilled thick plain yogurt
- 4 tablespoons sugar
- Pinch kosher salt
- 1½ to 2 cups chilled water or milk
- 6 ice cubes (optional)

1 Grind the cardamom seeds to a fine powder in a mortar and pestle or spice grinder, then add the mint leaves and grind as fine as possible.

2 Place the yogurt in a large mixing bowl. Using a whisk or an electric beater on low speed, beat the yogurt until it is completely smooth. Add the cardamom seed–mint mixture, sugar, and salt; blend well.

3 Add the chilled water or milk (more or less, depending on how thick you like your lassi), and keep beating until the consistency is smooth and a frothy layer forms on top.

4 Put the ice cubes (if using) in tall serving glasses and pour the lassi over the ice. Garnish with mint leaves and serve immediately.

Make It Healthier: You can reduce the fat content by using low-fat or fat-free yogurt.

Cooking Tip: Make a salted lassi by omitting the sugar and cardamom and adding 1 teaspoon rock salt, ½ teaspoon kosher salt, and some Roasted Cumin Powder (page 42).

CUMIN COOLER

Jal Jeera

ALL INDIA

VEGAN
GLUTEN-FREE
PEANUT-FREE
SOY-FREE
ALLIUM-FREE

SERVES 2 ◆ PREP TIME: 10 MINUTES Jal jeera *literally means "cumin water." Cumin is widely used in Indian cuisine for its medicinal properties. This drink is usually made in the summer, as it not only cools the body but also soothes the stomach in the season known to create indigestion and acidity.*

1 tablespoon Roasted Cumin Powder (page 42)
Seeds from 4 green cardamom pods (optional)
1 teaspoon fennel seeds (optional)
1½ teaspoons black salt or rock salt
½ cup mint leaves
1 tablespoon seedless tamarind pulp
5 peppercorns
1 teaspoon dried raw mango powder (amchur)
1 teaspoon chaat masala (optional)
Ice cubes (optional)
Chilled water or soda water

1 In a spice grinder or blender, combine the cumin powder, cardamom seeds (if using), fennel seeds (if using), and black salt. Process until the mixture resembles a fine powder. Add the mint leaves, tamarind, peppercorns, and mango powder, and process again. If the mixture is too dry, add 1 or 2 tablespoons of water to create a thick paste.

2 Add the chaat masala (if using) and blend again.

3 Strain the juices from this mixture through a fine-mesh sieve into two glasses. Add ice to the two glasses (if using) and top the concentrate with chilled water or soda water. Mix with a spoon to blend.

Cooking Tip: The paste can be made ahead and refrigerated in an airtight container for one day, or frozen in an ice cube tray for months.

Serving Tip: Jal jeera can be served as a digestive after a meal. Add a ½-inch piece of ginger to the paste for extra digestive properties.

ROASTED MANGO COOLER

Aam Panna Sharbat

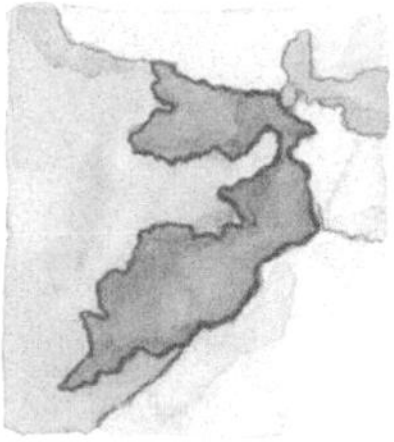

EAST INDIA

VEGAN
GLUTEN-FREE
PEANUT-FREE
SOY-FREE
ALLIUM-FREE

SERVES 5 TO 6 ◆ PREP TIME: 5 MINUTES ◆ COOK TIME: 20 TO 25 MINUTES

Aam panna is made and enjoyed throughout India during mango season, and has a lovely cooling effect. In this Bengali version of the drink, the mangoes are roasted first, creating a delightful, smoky flavor. For me, it makes the Indian summer something to look forward to.

- 2 medium green, firm mangoes (unripe)
- ½ cup sugar, divided, or more, depending on the tartness of the fruit
- ½ teaspoon black salt or rock salt
- 1 teaspoon Roasted Cumin Powder (page 42)
- 4 to 5 cups cold water

1 Using a fork, pierce the skin of the mangoes all over several times. Place the mangoes on a gas burner and turn the heat to medium. Turn the mangoes from time to time to ensure even blackening of the skin. This will take 15 to 20 minutes, depending on their size. Alternatively, to roast them in the oven, preheat it to 400°F, wrap the mangoes in aluminum foil, and cook for 25 to 30 minutes, depending on size.

2 Allow the mangoes to cool completely and then gently peel away the charred skin. The flesh inside should be warm and cooked through. Scrape all the pulp into a bowl and discard the seeds. If any of the mango flesh looks uncooked, discard it.

3 In a blender, combine the pulp, half the sugar, the salt, and the cumin powder; blend until smooth. With the motor still going, stream in the water and blend until fully incorporated. Taste and add all or part of the remaining sugar until you reach your desired sweetness. Blend until smooth. Serve.

Cooking Tip: You can make the mango concentrate in advance by following all the steps up to where you add the water. Refrigerate the concentrate for up to a week.

Make It Faster: Instead of roasting them, cook the mangoes in an electric pressure cooker for 10 minutes.

FENNEL SEED COOLER

Variyali Saunf Sharbat

WEST AND CENTRAL INDIA

VEGAN
GLUTEN-FREE
PEANUT-FREE
SOY-FREE
ALLIUM-FREE

SERVES 2 ◆ PREP TIME: 5 MINUTES, PLUS 1 HOUR TO SOAK *The Indian heat is responsible for some very interesting cooling beverages. This fennel seed drink from Gujarat instantly cools and refreshes the body. It is quite a fragrant drink, with the taste of the fennel shining through. It's perfect on a hot day or after an indulgent meal to aid digestion. To add a burst of flavor, squeeze half a lime into the mix.*

¼ cup fennel seeds, ground to a powder
1 whole clove, crushed with a mortar and pestle
2 tablespoons candy sugar, rock sugar, granulated sugar, or honey
2 cups cold water

1 Place the fennel seed powder and crushed clove in a tall glass and fill the glass with cold water. Let the spices soak for 1 hour.

2 Strain the spiced water through a fine-mesh sieve into a bowl, add the sugar, and mix well until the sugar is dissolved.

3 Pour equal amounts of the concentrate into two glasses and top them up with cold water. Serve.

Make It Healthier: To add to the digestive and cooling properties of this drink, add a pinch of freshly ground black pepper or cardamom.

MASALA CHAI

ALL INDIA

VEGETARIAN
EGG-FREE
GLUTEN-FREE
PEANUT-FREE
SOY-FREE
ALLIUM-FREE

SERVES 2 ♦ PREP TIME: 10 MINUTES ♦ COOK TIME: 5 MINUTES *Masala chai is one Indian specialty that I find wherever I travel throughout world. My recipe requires minimum effort, and the results are very rewarding. The best part is that you can alter the ratio of the spices to make your favorites shine through. The chai masala stores well for a month, so you can use, hoard, and share it as you please.*

FOR THE CHAI MASALA
1 teaspoon peppercorns (optional)
8 (1-inch) cinnamon sticks or pieces of cassia bark
5 whole cloves
2 tablespoons whole green cardamom pods
2 tablespoons fennel seeds
2 tablespoons ground ginger
1 teaspoon grated nutmeg (optional)
¼ cup dried chopped lemongrass (optional)
¼ cup dried rose petals (optional)

FOR THE TEA
2½ cups milk
4 teaspoons black tea leaves
Sugar

To make the chai masala

1 Heat a cast-iron skillet or tava over medium-high heat. When hot, add the peppercorns (if using), cinnamon, cloves, and cardamom. Dry roast, stirring constantly, until the spices become aromatic, about 5 minutes. Take care not to burn the spices; turn the heat to low if you're concerned. Transfer to a plate and allow to cool completely.

2 In a spice grinder or mortar and pestle, add the roasted ingredients, fennel seeds, ground ginger, and any of the optional spices you are using. Grind together until they are a fine powder.

3 Store in an airtight container in the refrigerator or a cool, dark place. *continued* ▸

To make the tea

1 In a saucepan, bring the milk to a simmer. Add the tea leaves and simmer. When the color of the milk changes, add the sugar and chai masala (about ½ tablespoon per cup of tea).

2 Simmer for about 1 minute, turn off the heat, and let the tea steep for about 1 minute.

3 Strain the tea into cups and adjust the sugar to your taste.

Make It Healthier: For a lighter version, use skim milk or reduce the amount of milk by half and use water for the rest.

Cooking Tip: You can use as little or as much of the chai masala as you like in your tea. Start with my recommendation and scale up slowly if you want a bigger flavor.

MIZORAM BANANA FRITTERS

Koat Pitha

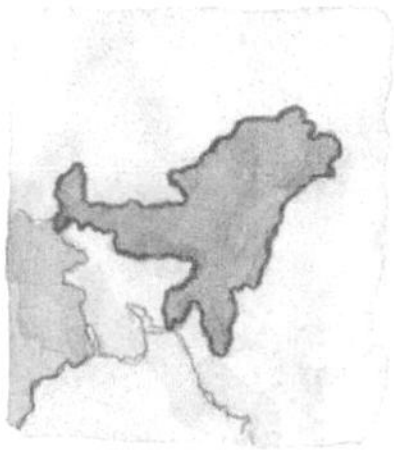

NORTHEAST INDIA

VEGAN
GLUTEN-FREE
PEANUT-FREE
SOY-FREE
ALLIUM-FREE

SERVES 2 ◆ PREP TIME: 5 MINUTES ◆ COOK TIME: 20 MINUTES *Northeast Indian cuisine is atypical, with flavors that are more organic, fresh, and simple than those found in other regions. Koat pitha, a typical banana fritter that is quite popular in the state of Mizoram, reflects this simplicity. It's really quick to make and delicious on its own, or served as a nibble with some Masala Chai* *(page 227).*

- ¾ cup powdered jaggery
- ¼ to ½ cup water
- 2 medium ripe or overripe bananas, mashed
- ¾ cup rice flour
- Vegetable oil for deep frying

1 In a saucepan over medium heat, melt the jaggery with the water until it forms a thick syrup. Strain this through a sieve into a large bowl to remove any scum that may rise to the top.

2 Add the mashed bananas and the rice flour to the bowl and mix well until it is well mixed and thick.

3 In a deep saucepan, heat about 2 inches of oil over medium-high heat until it begins to shimmer. Turn the heat to medium-low. Working in batches, drop tablespoons of the batter into the hot oil and fry them until golden brown, 7 to 10 minutes. Using a slotted spoon, transfer the cooked fritters to a paper towel–lined plate; serve warm.

Cooking Tip: For a taste twist, you can crush the seeds from two cardamom pods and add them to the batter, or add ¼ teaspoon of grated nutmeg.

COCONUT LADOO

ALL INDIA

FESTIVAL FOOD
VEGETARIAN
EGG-FREE
GLUTEN-FREE
PEANUT-FREE
SOY-FREE
ALLIUM-FREE

MAKES 10 TO 12 LADOOS ♦ PREP TIME: 5 MINUTES ♦ COOK TIME: 12 TO 15 MINUTES

Coconut ladoo combines two of my favorite ingredients—coconut and condensed milk—and is an absolute must-have in your Indian food repertoire when a sweet craving strikes. During the festival of lights, Diwali, easy-to-make ladoos like this are often part of the celebrations. The most difficult part about the recipe is stopping yourself from eating them all.

- 2 teaspoons ghee
- 1⅓ cups tightly packed fresh, or frozen and thawed, grated coconut, or 1¾ cup dried (desiccated) unsweetened coconut, divided
- 1 (14-ounce) can sweetened condensed milk
- 5 cardamom pods, seeded and crushed
- 1 tablespoon slivered nuts, such as almonds, pistachios, or cashews (optional)

1 In a small saucepan, melt the ghee over medium heat. Add 1 cup of coconut and stir for about 3 minutes to remove some moisture, but be careful not to brown the coconut. (If you're using dried coconut, skip this step and add 1½ cups of dried coconut directly to the condensed milk.)

2 In a medium saucepan over low heat, mix the condensed milk and cardamom seeds. Keep stirring to prevent sticking. When the mixture thickens and starts to pull away from the sides of the pan, after 10 to 12 minutes, transfer to a bowl and cool.

3 When the mixture has cooled, pinch a small to medium ball and roll it on your palm. It helps if your palm is slightly wet with water. Spread the remaining ⅓ cup of coconut (or ¼ cup of dried coconut) onto a plate. Roll the ball in the coconut until it is nicely coated. Repeat until you have used up all the batter.

4 Press a couple of slivered nuts (if using) onto each ladoo as a kind of jewel garnish. Serve immediately or store refrigerated for up to 4 days.

Serving Tip: Arrange these ladoos on an elegant plate for celebrations.

CARROT HALVA

Gaajar ka Halwa

NORTH INDIA

FESTIVAL FOOD
VEGETARIAN
EGG-FREE
GLUTEN-FREE
PEANUT-FREE
SOY-FREE
ALLIUM-FREE

SERVES 6 ♦ PREP TIME: 20 MINUTES ♦ COOK TIME: 1 HOUR *A* halwa *can be loosely defined as a dense, sweetened confection. It is made across the country with various ingredients, including carrots, semolina, and other fruits and vegetables. Carrot halva is typically made for festivals like Holi and Diwali. Traditionally, this dessert is cooked for hours, but I use this quicker stove-top recipe, which yields delicious results.*

- 5 to 6 medium red or orange carrots (if using orange carrots, you may need to add an extra ½ cup sugar)
- 4 tablespoons ghee
- 10 cashews, coarsely chopped
- 10 almonds, coarsely chopped
- 1 tablespoon raisins (optional)
- 2½ cups whole milk
- 1 cup sugar
- Seeds from 5 cardamom pods, removed and crushed to a powder
- 2 to 3 saffron strands (optional)

1 Rinse, peel, and grate the carrots finely by hand. (You could also use a food processor, but I find the texture and taste more appealing with hand-grated carrots.)

2 In a heavy saucepan or kadhai, heat the ghee. Add the chopped nuts and raisins (if using) and sauté on low heat until light golden brown. Remove and set aside in a bowl.

3 In the same ghee and pan, on medium-low heat, add the carrots and stir to coat for about 5 minutes. Add the milk and stir through. Allow the mixture to come to a simmer. Stir occasionally. The milk will be absorbed by the carrots and slowly reduce. Add the sugar and crushed cardamom seeds, and stir. You will find that the milk solids from the milk will naturally separate and stick to the sides of the pan; scrape them down frequently and stir them back into the carrot mix. This milk solid is known as khoya in India, and it adds a delicious creaminess to the final dish. *continued* ▸

4 Stir occasionally until the milk has reduced by 75 percent and the ghee is separating, 30 to 40 minutes. Add half the cooked nut mixture and mix thoroughly.

5 When the mixture looks almost dry, after about another 5 minutes, transfer to a serving platter or bowl. Garnish with the remaining nuts and saffron strands (if using). Serve hot or cool. The halva keeps fresh in the refrigerator for about a week.

Make It Faster: Follow the first three steps as written. Add half the nuts and transfer the mixture to the electric pressure cooker. Cook on high pressure for 8 minutes. Allow the pressure to release naturally before you open the pot. If the halva is runny, dry it more by returning the mix to the stove-top saucepan and cooking gently until the milk evaporates. Stir frequently at this stage. Garnish as in step 5.

Make It Easier: To make halva in a slow cooker, follow the first three steps through when you add the milk. Transfer this carrot, ghee, and milk mixture to the slow cooker, and add the sugar and cardamom. Cook for 3 hours on High. If the halva is runny, prop up a corner of the lid with the handle of a wooden spoon so it is slightly open and cook for another hour on Low. Stir occasionally to prevent the halva from drying up or burning.

PARSI WEDDING CUSTARD

Laganu Custard

WEST AND CENTRAL INDIA

VEGETARIAN
GLUTEN-FREE
PEANUT-FREE
SOY-FREE
ALLIUM-FREE

SERVES 4 ◆ PREP TIME: 10 MINUTES ◆ COOK TIME: 1 HOUR *This Indian specialty is easy to make, and the richness of the custard, combined with nutmeg and the distinctive charoli nut, gives it a unique appeal. I love the slightly blackened parts on top of the custard that impart a rich caramel flavor to the dish. This dessert is quite notorious for second and third helpings.*

- 4 cups whole milk
- 1 (14-ounce) can sweetened condensed milk, divided
- 1 tablespoon sugar
- 4 eggs
- 2 teaspoons vanilla extract
- ½ teaspoon grated nutmeg
- 2 tablespoons charoli nuts or almond or cashew slivers
- Unsalted butter, for greasing the tin and topping the custard

1 Preheat the oven to 400°F.

2 In a heavy saucepan over medium-high heat, bring the whole milk to a boil. As soon as the milk begins to boil, turn the heat to low and cook until the milk is reduced by almost half, stirring frequently to prevent scorching. This should take about 20 minutes.

3 Remove the pan from the heat and stir in half of the condensed milk and the sugar. Then return the pan to the stove over low heat and stir until the sugar has dissolved, about 5 minutes. Taste for sweetness. If you think you'd like it sweeter, pour in the rest of the condensed milk from the can and stir well. Remove the pan from the heat and set it aside to cool slightly.

4 In a large bowl, beat the eggs with a hand whisk or an electric beater until light but not too frothy. Add the sweetened milk mixture in a thin stream with one hand as you whisk it into the eggs with the other hand. This is important: If you don't aerate the eggs when the warm liquid is added, they may scramble. When all the milk is incorporated into the egg mixture, add the vanilla and nutmeg and continue to mix well. Add the nuts and mix well. continued ▶

5 Grease an 8-inch square baking dish or four individual ramekins and pour in the custard. Dot the top of the custard with tiny pieces of butter.

6 Bake for 30 to 40 minutes, or until the custard is set, the top is lightly browned, and a skewer inserted in the center comes out clean.

7 Remove the custard from the oven and set it aside to cool, then cut it into squares and serve, or refrigerate for later.

Make It Healthier: You can use low-fat milk for half the quantity of milk in the recipe.

Ingredient Tip: Charoli nuts are small, lentil-size, brown nuts with a distinctive flavor. Try to buy them at an Indian grocer or online. Almonds or cashews are good alternatives.

RICH MILK CAKE

Kalakand

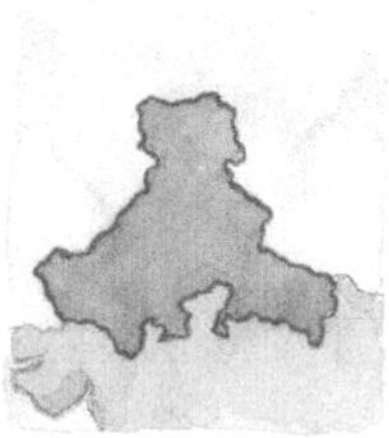

NORTH INDIA

FESTIVAL FOOD
VEGETARIAN
EGG-FREE
GLUTEN-FREE
PEANUT-FREE
SOY-FREE
ALLIUM-FREE

MAKES ONE 1-POUND CAKE ◆ PREP TIME: 10 MINUTES, PLUS 2 HOURS TO SET ◆ COOK TIME: 15 MINUTES *In the arid region of Rajasthan, where milk is an important source of hydration, this sweet is king. It is also commonly found across the country during festivals like Diwali, Holi, and Navratri.*

- 1 tablespoon ghee
- 12 ounces paneer, fresh or frozen and thawed, crumbled if fresh, grated if thawed
- 1 (14-ounce) can sweetened condensed milk
- Seeds from 8 cardamom pods, removed and crushed to a powder
- 6 to 8 strands saffron (optional)
- 12 pistachios, slivered
- 12 almonds or cashews, slivered
- 2 teaspoons rose water (optional)

1 Grease a flat plate or steel thali with the ghee.

2 In a heavy saucepan over low heat, mix together the crumbled paneer and condensed milk. Cook, stirring constantly, until the mixture begins to thicken and pull away from the sides of the pan. When the mixture starts to become one solid mass, after about 15 minutes, turn off the heat. Depending on the size of saucepan and the intensity of the heat, the time needed can vary.

3 Remove the pan from the heat and stir in the cardamom powder and saffron (if using). Pour the mixture onto the greased plate or thali and gently shake it from side to side or use a spatula to even the mix out. Gently press the nuts into the kalakand with the back of a spoon, covering the entire top. Sprinkle the rose water on top (if using), cover the batter with plastic wrap, and refrigerate for 2 hours until set.

4 Remove the kalakand from the refrigerator and slice it into diamonds or scoop it into bowls to serve.

Serving Tip: If you are serving the kalakand during Diwali, plate it on a traditional Indian tray or serving dish with lit votive candles or diyas, traditional clay oil lamps, lining the serving dish.

APPENDIX A

USING A PRESSURE COOKER

In this book, I use an electric Instant Pot 7-in-1 pressure cooker for the timings in the Make It Faster tips. If you own a stovetop pressure cooker, or a different model or type of electric pressure cooker, you'll need to modify the timing to suit your appliance.

If you are using an electric pressure cooker other than an Instant Pot, in most cases you can use the pressure setting, timing, and pressure release method specified in the tips. For instructions that call for the Meat Stew setting, select high pressure, and use the timing and pressure release instructions that are specified in the tips.

If you are using a stovetop pressure cooker, use the pressure setting, timing, and pressure release setting specified in the tips (and follow the previous instructions for tips that call for the Meat Stew setting). Turn the burner to high heat to bring the pressure cooker to the correct pressure. Once the cooker is at the correct pressure, begin timing and turn the burner down to the lowest setting that will maintain the correct pressure (usually medium-low or simmer). Use the pressure release method specified in the tips.

You can also check the manual that comes with your pressure cooker for information on appropriate timing, and I have found Linda Pazzaglia's website Hip Pressure Cooking (www.hippressurecooking.com) to be helpful, too.

COOKING DALS

In the olden days, and even in today's very traditional Indian kitchens, dals are cooked slowly over a low flame for many hours before the spices, tempering oils, and other flavors are added. This breaks down the dals and adds a creaminess to the final texture. However, in most modern homes, dals are cooked quickly in the pressure cooker, which reduces cooking time to a few minutes.

For the recipes in this book, I have broken the process of making dals into two easy steps for the pressure cooker. The first is boiling or cooking the dal, and the second is adding flavor to the cooked dal. This simple two-step process will greatly reduce the time you need to recreate these traditional, delicious dals at home.

FOR LENTILS

Lentils do not need to be soaked before cooking in the pressure cooker. Always remember to season lentils with kosher salt, ½ to 1 teaspoon of turmeric, and at least 2 teaspoons of vegetable oil to prevent frothing during cooking, which can be very messy. In the lentil recipes in this book, first cook the lentils in the pressure cooker according to the chart below (or by your estimation), and then proceed with the masala pastes and flavor bases as described in the recipes. I use enough water to cover the lentils by about 1 inch.

TYPE OF LENTILS	DRY, COOKING TIME (IN MINUTES)
Whole red lentils *(masoor)*	**15 to 20**
Split red lentils *(masoor dal)*	**15 to 20**
Yellow split mung beans *(moong dal)*	**15 to 20**
Pigeon peas *(tuvar dal)*	**15 to 20**
Black lentils *(urad dal)*	**15 to 20**
Split chickpeas *(channa dal)*	**15 to 20**

FOR BEANS

Dried beans will double in volume and weight after soaking or cooking. To avoid overflow in the inner pot, do not fill the inner pot with water above the half-full mark. The beans may be soaked for at least 4 hours or overnight, or cooked dry. When cooking all dried beans, be sure there is enough liquid in the pot to cover the beans.

In the bean recipes in this book, first cook the beans in the pressure cooker according to the chart below (or by your estimation, unless stated otherwise in the recipe), and then proceed with the masala pastes and flavor bases as described in the recipes.

TYPE OF BEANS	DRY, COOKING TIME (IN MINUTES)	SOAKED, COOKING TIME (IN MINUTES)
Black-eyed peas	20 to 25	15 to 20
Whole chickpeas *(chole, kabuli channa)*	35 to 40	15 to 20
Kidney beans, red	25 to 30	15 to 20
Dried white peas *(ragda vatana)*	20 to 25	15 to 20

APPENDIX B

MEASUREMENTS AND CONVERSIONS

VOLUME EQUIVALENTS (LIQUID)

US STANDARD	US STANDARD (OUNCES)	METRIC (APPROXIMATE)
2 tablespoons	1 fl. oz.	30 mL
¼ cup	2 fl. oz.	60 mL
½ cup	4 fl. oz.	120 mL
1 cup	8 fl. oz.	240 mL
1½ cups	12 fl. oz.	355 mL
2 cups or 1 pint	16 fl. oz.	475 mL
4 cups or 1 quart	32 fl. oz.	1 L
1 gallon	128 fl. oz.	4 L

OVEN TEMPURATURES

FAHRENHEIT	CELSIUS (APPROXIMATE)
250°F	120°C
300°F	150°C
325°F	165°C
350°F	180°C
375°F	190°C
400°F	200°C
425°F	220°C
450°F	230°C

VOLUME EQUIVALENTS (DRY)

US STANDARD	METRIC (APPROXIMATE)
⅛ teaspoon	1 mL
¼ teaspoon	2 mL
1 teaspoon	5 mL
1 tablespoon	15 mL
¼ cup	59 mL
⅓ cup	79 mL
½ cup	118 mL
1 cup	235 mL

WEIGHT EQUIVALENTS

US STANDARD	METRIC (APPROXIMATE)
½ ounce	15 g
1 ounce	30 g
2 ounces	60 g
4 ounces	115 g
8 ounces	225 g
12 ounces	340 g
16 ounces or 1 pound	455 g

ACKNOWLEDGMENTS

This book has been possible with the help of so many people and forces. I'd like to thank my editor, Clara Song Lee. While most would commission a book on Indian food classics, you took a leap of faith by allowing me to present an unsung, beautiful aspect of the cuisine—India's regional food gems. I'm thankful to the talented team at Rockridge Press, Beth Heidi Adelman and Katherine Green, for putting so much effort into making this book shine.

In the course of writing it, I would cross-check the authenticity of recipes with friends and in the process hear beautiful personal anecdotes that made the food stories richer. For their contributions, I am grateful. It has made me realize that Mumbai is a true melting pot of so many Indian communities.

Finally I would like to thank my husband, Prasanna, for his eagerness to be my food taster and his unwavering faith in me. Thank you to our angel, Meiko, who keeps me sane. I am so fortunate that Emery, our darling daughter, accompanied me on my journey of writing this book and was born right after I completed its work. And a special bow of gratitude to my late grandfather Walter Netto, who encouraged me to be everything I could be.

RESOURCES

GROCERY STORES AND ONLINE RETAILERS

AMAZON.COM ONLINE RETAILER www.amazon.com

BOB'S RED MILL NATURAL FOODS www.bobsredmill.com

GROCERY BABU ONLINE INDIAN GROCERY STORE www.grocerybabu.com

INDIAN BLEND ONLINE GROCERY STORE www.indianblend.com

ISHOPINDIAN.COM ONLINE INDIAN RETAILER www.ishopindian.com

KALUSTYAN'S FINE SPECIALTY FOODS kalustyans.com

KHANAPAKANA ONLINE INDIAN GROCERY STORE shop.khanapakana.com

NAMASTE PLAZA INDIAN SUPERMARKET www.namasteplaza.com

PATEL BROTHERS INDIAN GROCERY STORES store.patelbros.com

PENZEYS SPICES www.penzeys.com

WORLD SPICE MERCHANTS www.worldspice.com

To find brick-and-mortar Indian grocery stores in your area, search on Google.com or Yelp.com, or refer to the US Indian grocery store directory at www.thokalath.com/grocery/.

RECIPE INDEX

P

Q

R

S

T

V

REGIONAL INDEX

SOUTH INDIA

WEST AND CENTRAL INDIA

INDEX

M

N

O

P